# The Ginnie Mae Manual

# The Ginnie Mae Manual

GNMA Mortgage-Backed Securities
Dealers Association

**DOW JONES-IRWIN**  Homewood, Illinois  60430

# Foreword and Acknowledgments

This manual is presented as a reference work on Ginnie Maes. These relatively new Pass-Through securities have grown in capital-market importance since their introduction in 1970.

## Acknowledgments

To assure an ethical and professional-quality manual on Ginnie Mae securities, the GNMA Mortgage-Backed Securities Dealers Association employed a nationally known public relations firm to research and assist with preparation of this reference work. The Association's education committee conducted in-depth research, analysis, field contacts, and review of all available literature during this comprehensive examination of Ginnie Mae Pass-Throughs.

In the course of their study, the Association's education committee and personnel of the assisting firm contacted responsible experts among money managers in all major investor categories (commercial banks, credit unions, mortgage bankers, retirement-pension funds, savings banks, and savings and loan associations), securities brokers, investment bankers, a leading public accounting firm, the academic community, and governmental and professional associations.

We want to express our thanks to all those who contributed their encouragement.

*December 1977*

# Contents

# 1

# Ginnie Maes—
# An Attractive
# Investment Opportunity

Ginnie Mae securities offer the best available yields of all actively traded U.S. government instruments. These bond-type vehicles combine the best features of both mortgages and government bonds: safety, attractive yield, cash flow, and superior marketability.

One piece of paper—a negotiable Ginnie Mae certificate—gives investors a pro rata share of a pool of first-mortgage loans. Thus Ginnie Maes are capital-market instruments that permit private-sector investors to support the nation's housing industry. This helps keep the interest costs paid by home buyers at reasonable levels and augments the flow of new investment funds into home building.

Over the past six years extensive primary and secondary markets in Ginnie Mae pass-throughs have been built up. Members of the GNMA Mortgage-Backed Securities Dealers Association furnish technical guidance and trade the securities at net prices. These dealers also take sizable market positions, train client personnel, and provide investment advice.

The first sale of Ginnie Maes was made on February 19,

1970, to a state public employees' retirement fund. As of September 30, 1977, the value of all issued Ginnie Mae securities amounted to $47.3 billion. Based on the new-issues rate, established over the first nine months of 1977, it is anticipated that by year-end the total outstanding value will be in excess of $50 billion.

The prime aim of this manual is to explain the investment attributes of Ginnie Maes. For example, Section 4.D takes up the "Administrative Simplicity" of handling Ginnie Maes and Section 8.J discusses "Bookkeeping Methods."

Throughout the text, *Ginnie Mae* is used to designate the security and *GNMA* refers to the Government National Mortgage Association.

# 2

# Background of the Government National Mortgage Association (GNMA)

## A. REASON FOR CREATION

In 1968, Congress established the Government National Mortgage Association (GNMA) to help finance needed housing by making real estate mortgages attractive to all types of investors, regardless of their previous mortgage experience. Pursuant to the provisions of the Housing Act of 1968, GNMA developed a new type of mortgage-backed security—the pass-through Ginnie Mae—which represents a pool or package of mortgages insured by either the Federal Housing Administration (FHA) or the Farmers Home Administration (FmHA) or guaranteed by the Veterans Administration (VA). GNMA guarantees the timely payment of principal and interest on these securities. The GNMA guaranty is backed by the full faith and credit of the U.S. government.

## B. HISTORY

*Department of Housing and Urban Development* (HUD).
The Government National Mortgage Association, a government corporation, is a part of HUD.

3

*National Mortgage Association* (National Housing Act of 1938).

Created Federal National Mortgage Association (FNMA).

*National Mortgage Association* (National Housing Act of 1940).

1. Authorized FNMA to purchase and sell mortgages.

2. Authorized the Federal Housing Administration (FHA) to insure mortgages.

*Veterans Administration* (legislation enacted in 1948).

Authorized the Veterans Administration (VA) to guarantee mortgages.

*National Mortgage Association* (National Housing Act of 1954).

Redefined and expanded FNMA functions to include: (1) conducting secondary-market operations; (2) providing special assistance when adequate home-financing resources are lacking; (3) performing management and liquidating functions on selected mortgages.

FNMA partitioned into FNMA and *Government National Mortgage Association* (GNMA) (Housing and Urban Development Act of 1968).

FNMA (1968)—private investors took over ownership; performs secondary-market operations.

GNMA (1968)—remained a government corporation as part of HUD.

1. *The special assistance function.* The traditional function consists of: (a) the purchase of selected types of FHA- or FmHA-insured and VA-guaranteed mortgages to assist low- and middle-income homeowners; (b) the support of home construction activity during declines in private mortgage lending. The emergency function consists of the purchase of FHA- or FmHA-insured, VA-guaranteed, and conventional mortgages to stimulate home buying and home construction for a limited period of time. GNMA is not authorized to originate new mortgages.

The Emergency Home Purchase Assistance Act of 1974

expanded the special assistance function to include the purchase of GNMA/FHLMC (Federal Home Loan Mortgage Corporation) conventional home mortgages administered through the facilities of FHLMC.

2. *The mortgage-backed securities function.* GNMA is authorized to guarantee the timely payment of principal and interest on long-term securities that are backed by self-liquidating pools of mortgages. Pass-through–type and bond-type securities are eligible for guaranty.

Pass-through securities—Ginnie Maes—are issued exclusively by FHA/VA-approved mortgagees, primarily mortgage bankers and thrift institutions. These securities are not guaranteed by the issuer. However, the issuer is the primary obligor and is contractually bound to perform a series of administrative functions specified in GNMA's "Mortgage-Backed Securities Guide" (HUD Handbook, GNMA 5500.1C).

Ginnie Maes are backed by pools of single-family or multi-family mortgages or projects under construction and by mobile home loans insured by FHA under Title I of the National Housing Act. A limited number of Ginnie Mae issues have been collateralized and insured by FmHA for rural housing.

Though a few bond-type issues were brought to market in 1972 and the first half of 1973, none have been issued or guaranteed since then.

3. *The management and liquidation function.* This function consists of the administration of a portfolio of FHA-insured mortgages acquired from FNMA upon the creation of GNMA.

# 3

# Perspective

## A. BROAD INVESTMENT APPEAL

The Ginnie Mae mortgage-backed security offers potential interest for a broad range of investors, including savings and loan associations, savings banks, retirement and pension funds, commercial banks, credit unions, and private individuals.

A Ginnie Mae certificate represents a pro rata share in a pool or package of FHA- or FmHA-insured or VA-guaranteed mortgages. Ginnie Mae certificates representing these pools are described as pass-throughs. The issuer of the certificate collects the amortization-of-principal amount and interest on all mortgages in the pool and passes these sums through to the Ginnie Mae investors.

Two types of pass-throughs are authorized, namely participation certificates and modified pass-throughs (formerly called fully modified pass-throughs). Modified pass-throughs are generally referred to as pass-throughs. Although participation certificates have been authorized, none are outstanding at present.

This manual is primarily concerned with pass-throughs

collateralized by single-family mortgages on one- to four-unit dwellings. However, certificates are also issued for pools of project mortgages.

Ginnie Mae securities are available only in registered form. However, they are freely transferable and assignable. They are negotiable securities which can be bought and sold in the

**FIGURE 3-1**
**The Ginnie Mae Mortgage-Backed Securities Process**

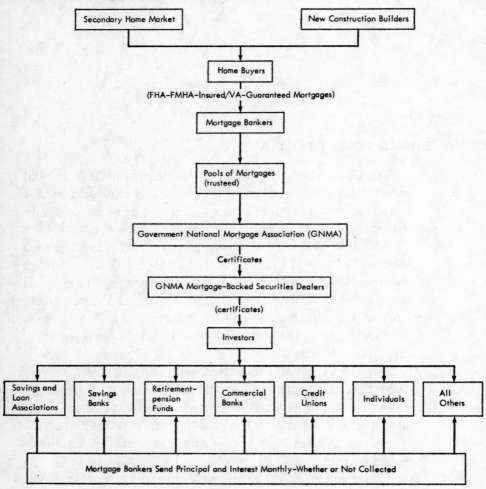

same manner as other registered securities, such as common stocks or corporate bonds.

To promote clarity and accuracy in its statistical presentations, this manual employs the investor classifications used by GNMA. These classifications are shown in Figure 3-1, which depicts the Ginnie Mae mortgage-backed securities process.

## B. SAFETY

In the event of any deficiencies of principal or interest, GNMA guarantees the timely payment of all amounts due to the certificate holder. This guaranty is backed by the full faith and credit of the U.S. government.

The statement generally used in conjunction with new issues of Ginnie Maes is:

> Timely payment of principal of and interest on the securities is guaranteed by GNMA pursuant to Section 306(g) of Title III of the National Housing Act. Section 306(g) provides that "The full faith and credit of the United States is pledged to the payment of all amounts which may be required to be paid under any guaranty under this subsection," and an opinion dated December 9, 1969, of an Assistant Attorney General of the United States states that such guarantees under Section 306(g) of mortgage-backed securities of the type referred to above "constitute general obligations of the United States backed by its full faith and credit."

The guarantee of the Government National Mortgage Association is facilitated by its ability to borrow from the United States Treasury, funds required to meet obligations under its guarantee. See Exhibit A (page 84) for the letter of February 13, 1970 from the Secretary of the Treasury. The opinion letter dated December 9, 1969 from an Assistant Attorney General of the United States is shown as Exhibit B (page 85). Together these documents confirm the full faith and credit guarantee of GNMA and show the source of funds available to provide any cash required under the guarantee. The GNMA guaranty applies to pass-through securities, participation certificates, and serial notes. Straight pass-through securities, which are no longer issued, do not carry GNMA's guaranty of *timely* payment of principal and interest. Payment on straight pass-throughs is made as collected.

In the unlikely situation that an issuer cannot make payment on pass-throughs, GNMA is obligated to provide the required funds. It also has the authority to reassign the mortgage servicing on the pool.

Figure 3-2 presents a simplified picture of the Ginnie Mae guaranty process.

**FIGURE 3-2**
**The Ginnie Mae Guaranty Process**

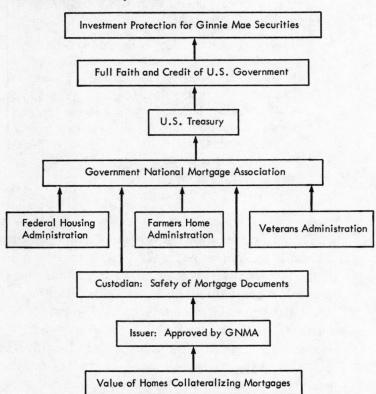

# 4

# Advantages of
# Ginnie Mae Securities

## A. OVERVIEW

From an investment viewpoint, the most important attributes of the Ginnie Mae are that it combines the characteristics of residential mortgages with those of fixed-income securities and that it provides the yield advantage normally associated with mortgage investments. Moreover, this security/mortgage hybrid combines the safety of government bonds with the advantages of a diversified portfolio.

This section analyzes the specific advantages of Ginnie Maes: yield, marketability, administrative simplicity, continuous cash flow, diversification, legal eligibility, the social benefits conferred by Ginnie Maes, and the competitive strengths of Ginnie Maes as compared to long-term governments and high-grade corporate bonds.

## B. YIELD

Security yields are a function of the stated interest rate and the price. Yields on pass-throughs are obtained from a "net yield table" which takes into account the unique features of Ginnie Maes. The most commonly used table is the Financial Publishing Company's "Net Yield Table for GNMA Mortgage-Backed Securities."

Yields on pass-throughs are calculated on two bases—the "yield-to-maturity" basis and the "12-year prepayment" basis. The yield-to-maturity basis indicates what an investor's return would be if all of the pooled mortgages were amortized over the full term of the mortgages. This is an unrealistic assumption, however, because there are usually prepayments on mortgages before the full term is completed.

Although it is not possible to precisely forecast mortgage prepayment rates for any specific pool, empirical data developed by the Federal Housing Administration from prepayment and default experience on FHA loans over a period of years has established the concept of prepayment in approximately 12 years for a 30-year, single-family mortgage. The convention used in the valuation of Ginnie Maes is that a single FHA, FmHA, or VA mortgage in a pool has a propensity to prepay during the 12th year of its life and that the entire pool therefore has the same propensity. For 30-year single-family pools, 12 years is often referred to as the "half-life" of the pool. This is a bond term which implies that half of the original principal amount may be returned through prepayment by the end of the 12th year. This 12-year prepayment basis for calculating yields on 30-year single-family Ginnie Maes is almost universally used. However, actual prepayment experience on GNMA pools varies widely. Although the oldest pools have existed for only seven years, it is evident that some are prepaying at a rate in excess of 300 percent of FHA experience. When such pools are purchased at a discount (that is, priced at less than the par value), the comparative investment return is higher than is generally recognized by the financial community.

Another reason for the underestimation of the comparative yields on Ginnie Maes is the failure to take into account the compounding effect of monthly payments upon yield. Since most bonds pay interest semiannually, adjustment factors must be used to equate their yields with Ginnie Mae yields. The values in Table 4-1 were taken from "Financial Pass-Through Yield and Value Tables for GNMA Mortgage-Backed Bonds."[1]

**TABLE 4-1**

| Ginnie Mae Yield | Add for Semiannual Bond Equivalent |
| --- | --- |
| 6.73 to 7.07 | 0.10% |
| 7.08 to 7.39 | 0.11 |
| 7.40 to 7.71 | 0.12 |
| 7.72 to 8.01 | 0.13 |
| 8.02 to 8.30 | 0.14 |
| 8.31 to 8.58 | 0.15 |
| 8.59 to 8.85 | 0.16 |
| 8.86 to 9.11 | 0.17 |

## C. MARKETABILITY

To understand the perspective from which this manual views marketability, the terms *marketability, negotiability,* and *security* must be defined.

1. *Marketability.* This characteristic represents the capacity of the market in a particular security to absorb a reasonable amount of buying and selling at reasonable price changes. Marketable securities are often said to be liquid, meaning that such securities can readily be converted into cash (liquidated) on short notice. Marketable securities have a broad appeal to investors, thus causing securities dealers to engage in active trading of the various issues involved. Pass-throughs possess a high degree of marketability due to the existence of large, active primary (new-issue) and secondary (trading) markets.

---

[1] Financial Publishing Company, Boston, Mass.

2. *Negotiability.* Under the Universal Commercial Code, a negotiable security is an instrument that can be transferred by endorsement or delivery. A Ginnie Mae is assignable and transferable, hence a negotiable security.

3. *Security.* A security in the sense that this manual uses the term is a common or preferred stock, a bond, a U.S. government or agency issue, or a state or municipal obligation. This differs from the sense in which the term is used in real estate practice, where "security" represents collateral given, deposited, or pledged to secure the fulfillment of an obligation or the payment of a debt.

Pass-throughs are currently among the most marketable of all securities. The prime reasons for the popularity of Ginnie Maes are their safety and attractive yields, combined with the existence of heavy secondary trading that assures a ready market for their purchase and sale.

## 1. Types of Investors

The rapid growth of the Ginnie Mae secondary market since 1971 has stemmed from the active interest in these securities among a wide array of investors and from the liquidity that GNMA dealers have created in the secondary market.

Savings banks and savings and loan associations were early buyers of Ginnie Maes because they were already familiar with direct investments in mortgages and because they were quick to recognize the many investment advantages offered by mortgage-backed, government-guaranteed securities. As the attributes of Ginnie Maes became better known, non-traditional mortgage investors, such as pension funds, commercial banks, and credit unions, became active buyers and traders of these securities.

The diversity of recent investor interest in Ginnie Maes is illustrated by Table 4-2.

**TABLE 4-2**
**Estimated Share of Ginnie Mae Purchases by Type of Institution, September 30, 1977**

| Investor | Percentage of Securities Held |
|---|---|
| Savings and loan associations . . . . . . . . . . . . . . . . . . . . . | 15.63 % |
| Savings banks . . . . . . . . . . . . . . . . . . . . . . . . . . . . . . | 12.20 |
| Retirement and pension funds . . . . . . . . . . . . . . . . . . . . | 10.85 |
| Commercial banks . . . . . . . . . . . . . . . . . . . . . . . . . . . . | 5.90 |
| Credit unions . . . . . . . . . . . . . . . . . . . . . . . . . . . . . . . | 2.65 |
| Individuals . . . . . . . . . . . . . . . . . . . . . . . . . . . . . . . | 1.01 |
| Mortgage and investment bankers*† . . . . . . . . . . . . . . . . | 19.66 |
| All others (including nominees)† . . . . . . . . . . . . . . . . . | 32.10 |
| Total . . . . . . . . . . . . . . . . . . . . . . . . . . . . . . . . . | 100.0% |
| | |
| Volume of outstanding securities held . . . . . . . . . . . . . . . | $47.27 billion |

*Includes securities in transfer and securities held in customer accounts.
†GNMA estimates that 13-14 percent in these two categories are owned by pension funds, held in street names and/or the names of nominees.
Source: Government National Mortgage Association.

## 2. The Role of the GNMA Dealer in Maintaining Marketability

Secondary market-making in Ginnie Maes has expanded significantly in recent years. These securities have staked out an expanding position in U.S. capital markets on a nationwide scale. Though the volume of secondary-market transactions is not kept, a volume figure can be estimated on the basis of some multiple of reregistrations. Based on GNMA estimates, the secondary-market volume in 1976 was $57 billion. (Statistics on Ginnie Mae markets are analyzed in detail in Section 6.) A key factor in the marketability of passthroughs has been the dealer community's extensive securities distribution system. Through their continuous contacts with institutional clients, their own principal-transaction positions, their flexible trading methods, and their high-speed communications networks, Ginnie Mae dealers have created a most efficient securities market.

## D. ADMINISTRATIVE SIMPLICITY

From an administrative standpoint, the purchase of Ginnie Maes is far simpler than the purchase of residential mortgages.

The Ginnie Mae investor is concerned with only one piece of paper—the certificate that represents a portion of an FHA/FmHA-insured or VA-guaranteed mortgage pool. The certificate issuer retains total responsibility for servicing the underlying mortgages and administering the necessary paperwork. In this way, the certificate holder avoids direct mortgage ownership, with its associated operating problems, responsibilities, and expense.

A pass-through purchase, unlike a direct investment in mortgages, eliminates such administrative problems as the following:

1. Investigating individual requests for mortgage loans to determine the credit standing of the borrower; the size, location, and quality of the property; the validity of supporting documents; and so on.
2. Collecting mortgage payments; maintaining tax, insurance, and payment records; following up delinquencies; and so on.
3. Collecting late payments and processing foreclosures.

In addition to eliminating the time and effort entailed in performing such administrative functions, pass-through securities permit operating savings. In view of rising labor and rental costs, the option of bypassing mortgage-department operating expense is a worthwhile consideration for investors in mortgages. "Clearly, the GNMA mortgage-backed security offers strong economic incentives to the lender to invest in this financial instrument rather than continue the cumbersome and costly direct investment in single-family mortgages."[2]

---

[2] Phillip C. Kidd, "GNMA Mortgage-Backed Security: The Wave of the Future," *Mortgage Banker*, April 1970.

In fact, purchasing pass-through securities is so simple that the prospective investor does not even have to possess prior real estate experience. His responsibilities are limited to non-technical bookkeeping functions which may be performed manually once a month. (See Section 8.J, "Bookkeeping Methods.")

## E. CONTINUOUS CASH FLOW

The steady, monthly cash flow of interest and amortization of principal provided by Ginnie Maes is a distinct advantage for some investors.

Interest and principal are paid to investors in pass-throughs on the 15th of each month for debt service due from the prior month (for example, interest and principal due on the mortgages January 1 are paid to the security holder on February 15).

The fact that interest is paid monthly rather than semi-annually, as is the case for most bonds, gives the investor a higher yield because of the compounding of the 12 monthly payments. This can produce an additional 10 to 17 basis points of return, depending on yield levels (see Section 4.B).

## F. LEGAL ELIGIBILITY

Due to backing of the full faith and credit of the U.S. government, Ginnie Maes can be used:

1.  As collateral against Treasury tax and loan accounts.
2.  For commercial bank advances and rediscounts at Federal Reserve banks.
3.  As security for public monies of the U.S. government.
4.  As pledges against public funds.
5.  As riskless assets for investments in state and local trusts.
6.  As real estate qualifying assets of savings and loan association and mutual savings banks.
7.  As acceptable assets for many institutions which are subject to statutory restrictions on other debt instruments.

8. As an acceptable mortgage-market investment for certain institutions previously restricted to the purchase of U.S. government or agency securities.

Table 4-3 is a state-by-state breakdown of the legal status of investments in Ginnie Maes by savings and loan associations, credit unions, banks, and insurance companies.

**TABLE 4-3**
**Authorization of Investments in Ginnie Maes by State Regulatory Authorities**

| State | Savings and Loan Associations | Credit Unions | Banks | Insurance Companies |
|---|---|---|---|---|
| Alabama | + | + | None | + |
| Alaska | None | None | + | + |
| Arizona | + | + | None | |
| Arkansas | + | + | None | |
| California | + | + | | |
| Colorado | + | | None | + |
| Connecticut | + | + | + | + |
| Delaware | Not authorized | None | Limited to 25 percent of aggregate capital | + |
| Florida | + | + | + | + |
| Georgia | + | + | + | + |
| Hawaii | Up to 30 percent of capital | None | 25 percent of deposits | |
| Idaho | | | | |
| Illinois | + | + | None | |
| Indiana | + | + | + | + |
| Iowa | + | + | + | + |
| Kansas | + | + | None | |
| Kentucky | + | + | + | + |
| Louisiana | + | | | + |
| Maine | + | + | + | |
| Maryland | + | + | + | + |
| Massachusetts | + | + | + | + |
| Michigan | + | + | None | + |
| Minnesota | + | + | + | + |
| Mississippi | | | | |
| Missouri | + | + | + | + |
| Montana | Cannot exceed 10 percent of assets | Not authorized | Not authorized | + |
| Nebraska | + | + | None | + |
| Nevada | + | None | None | |

**TABLE 4-3** *(continued)*

| State | Savings and Loan Associations | Credit Unions | Banks | Insurance Companies |
|---|---|---|---|---|
| New Hampshire . . . | + | + | + | + |
| New Jersey . . . . . | + | + | + | |
| New Mexico . . . . . | + | + | + | |
| New York . . . . . . | + | + | + | + |
| North Carolina . . . | + | + | None | + |
| North Dakota . . . . | | | | + |
| Ohio . . . . . . . . | + | Per individual request | + | |
| Oklahoma . . . . . . | + | + | None | + |
| Oregon . . . . . . . | + | + | None | + |
| Pennsylvania . . . . | + | + | + | |
| Rhode Island . . . . | + | + | + | + |
| South Carolina . . . | + | + | + | |
| South Dakota . . . . | + | None | None | |
| Tennessee . . . . . . | None | + | None | By statute |
| Texas . . . . . . . . | + | + | + | + |
| Utah . . . . . . . . | + | + | + | + |
| Vermont . . . . . . . | + | + | + | |
| Virginia . . . . . . | + | Not authorized | None | + |
| Washington . . . . . | + | + | + | |
| West Virginia . . . . | + | + | + | |
| Wisconsin . . . . . . | + | + | + | + |
| Wyoming . . . . . . | + | None | + | + |

+ = Authorized investment.
None = There are no state-regulated institutions.

## G.  SOCIAL BENEFITS

Ginnie Maes have made it possible for many institutions to support medium- and low-cost housing. They have also enabled institutions to identify themselves with their local economies by purchasing pass-throughs specifically backed by mortgages in their own areas. Such tailored investments encourage local home building. Typical high-profile "local image" or "trade-oriented" investors include public funds and local banks, savings and loan associations, credit unions, insurance companies, pension funds, and labor unions.

Moreover, through the growth of mortgage-backed securities, the nation's capital markets have directed billions of dollars into the mortgage market that might otherwise have been invested elsewhere. Thus pass-throughs have broadened the opportunity for the capital markets to support better housing in the nation.

An important consideration at this point is the convenience with which local institutions can invest in local real estate developments without direct investment in mortgages as such. Since investments in Ginnie Maes are the same as investments in other negotiable securities and possess such previously mentioned advantages as safety, high yields, and legal eligibility, these investments enable local institutions to confer local social benefits without forgoing fiscal responsibility.

Some institutions may even be able to promote their own welfare through the purchase of pass-throughs.

> The GNMA (Ginnie Mae) security is flexible and can be designed to benefit a fund's interests. If the fund wants the underlying mortgages to be on homes in a certain geographical area, for example, to help the fund's own members receive mortgage financing—this can be arranged. For example, some union funds restrict purchases to mortgages on union-built homes; some state employee funds restrict purchases to mortgages on homes within their state.[3]

John Evans, former director of the AFL-CIO department of urban affairs has said,

> Pension funds control tremendous resources in a nation where serious concern is being expressed about the rapid deterioration in the quality of American life, where we fall further behind in such areas as low- and moderate-income housing. Can a $370 billion giant shy away from confronting such concerns, when its dollars could play a tremendous role in their amelioration? While granting the need for various types of investments in a pension fund portfolio, the low ratio of mortgage investment by pension funds seems something of a mystery, particularly for those funds representing the construction industry.[4]

---

[3] Jerome L. Howard, "Mortgages Seen as Good Investments for Pension Fund Managers," *Mortgage Banker*, December 1975.
[4] Ibid.

## H.  COMPETITIVE STRENGTHS

Relative to Treasury bonds and high-grade corporate bonds, Ginnie Maes can provide money managers with selective advantages that improve portfolio performance.

From the quality or safety criterion, pass-throughs have a credit status comparable to that of Treasury bonds since both types of securities are backed by the full faith and credit of the U.S. government. An additional credit consideration for Ginnie Maes is the underlying collateral, which represents insured or guaranteed pooled mortgages.

The prime competitive strength of Ginnie Maes, as compared to Treasury bonds, is the more attractive yield of Ginnie Maes under certain capital-market conditions. Yields on Ginnie Maes have generally been the best available among actively traded government securities. Ginnie Maes' monthly cash flow (see Section 4.B) also provides some advantage over Treasury bonds which pay interest semiannually.

Some market authorities believe that the favorable yield of Ginnie Maes as compared to that of other government vehicles has been due to the comparative newness of these mortgage-backed instruments in the U.S. capital markets. A likelier explanation, however, is that the spread in yields has arisen from the inherent antipathy of the investment community to a new security with characteristics that deviate from the norm.

The marketability and legal eligibility of Ginnie Maes and Treasury bonds are about equal. Of course, their suitability depends upon the portfolio requirements of each individual investor.

The overriding competitive strength of Ginnie Maes, as compared to high-grade corporate bonds, is the full faith and credit guaranty of the U.S. government. Ginnie Maes are considered by most market experts to be safer investments than high-grade corporate bonds.

Despite this guaranty, at certain times the yields on Ginnie Maes have run 50 to 150 basis points over those of certain

corporate obligations. Yield relationships between Ginnie
Maes and corporate bonds have varied widely over time (see
Figure 4-1 below).

**FIGURE 4-1**
Ginnie Mae Yield Chart

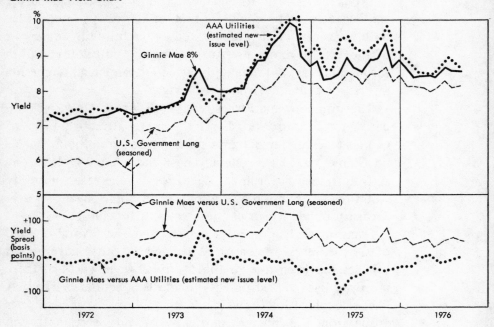

Another important advantage of pass-throughs over high-
grade corporate bonds is the legal eligibility of pass-throughs
as investments for many fiduciaries who are not permitted
to buy corporate bonds.

Due to such factors as their high safety rating, their higher
yields, and their large secondary-market volume, Ginnie Maes
offer portfolio managers greater marketability than that of
corporate bonds. Moreover, corporate obligations, unlike
Ginnie Maes, normally pay interest on a semiannual basis and
generally do not pay the principal until maturity.

# 5

# Pass-Through Ginnie Mae Securities

## A. DESCRIPTION

Pass-throughs—the term which this manual uses to designate fully modified pass-through securities on pools of single-family home mortgages—provide for a monthly fixed payment of principal and interest to security holders, whether or not the amount paid out to security holders has been collected on the mortgages. Prepayments and foreclosure proceeds are passed along to security holders as received.

As was noted above, there are several types of fully guaranteed pass-through securities. Two of these, the straight pass-through and the partially modified pass-through, have been inactive in recent years and will probably not be issued again.

According to GNMA regulations, the straight pass-through furnishes holders of the security with monthly payments of principal and interest, as collected, on the mortgages in the pool backing the security. The partially modified pass-through provides a set monthly interest payment, whether or not it is collected. Prepayments on the mortgages are passed through to the security holders in either case.

### 1. Single-Family Fully Modified Pass-Throughs

Some characteristics of single-family fully modified pass-throughs are:

1. Minimum pool size—$1 million.
2. Maturity generally 30 years, dated on the first of the month and maturing on the 15th.
3. Each pool issued by a specific FHA-approved mortgagee.
4. Minimum denomination of original face amount $25,000, with increments of $5,000.
5. For completeness and accuracy, a pass-through description includes:
   a. The name, address, and tax identification number of the security holder (registered owner).
   b. The GNMA pool number.
   c. The certificate number.
   d. The security interest rate (the annual interest rate of the certificate).
   e. The original principal amount of the certificate.
   f. The initial payment date.
   g. The maturity date.

### 2. Other Types of GNMA-Guaranteed Mortgage-Backed Securities

Other types of mortgage-backed securities guaranteed by GNMA are:

1. Construction loan certificates (CLCs)—collateralized by a construction loan advance on a project insured by FHA. The CLC pays *interest only* on a monthly basis until maturity. At that time, the CLC is replaced by a project loan certificate.
2. Project loans—loans generally similar to those on single-family houses, with one major exception—namely, that the pool may contain only one project mortgage, which is insured by the FHA under the National Housing Act.

Typical projects include multifamily dwellings, nursing homes, hospitals, and mobile home parks. The minimum pool size is $500,000.

3. Mobile home loans—loans collateralized by pools of 12- to 20-year FHA Title I mortgages or VA mobile home mortgages. The minimum pool size is $500,000.

4. Serial issues—issues secured by $5 million pools of 200 certificates, each in the amount of $25,000 and each with a different maturity and subject to prepayment.

5. GNMA bonds—GNMA/FHLB or GNMA/FNMA participation certificates. This guaranty authority has not been used during the past several years.

## B. ORIGINATION

Origination is the process by which the pooled mortgages secured by real property are brought into being. Since mortgage bankers originate the vast majority of such mortgages, mortgage bankers will be designated throughout this manual as the originators even though savings and loan associations and savings banks also originate mortgages.

Mortgages that are pooled to back Ginnie Mae securities may not have been insured (FHA) or guaranteed (VA) for more than one year on the date GNMA issues its commitment to guarantee the pool involved.

### 1. The Mortgage Banker

A mortgage banker is essentially a middleman between builders, developers, real estate brokers, and home buyers who specializes in originating mortgage loans for sale to permanent investors. As a local representative of regional or national institutional lenders, he acts as a correspondent between lenders and borrowers. Frequently he continues to service the loans he has sold.

In originating loans to pool for new mortgage-backed securities, a mortgage banker usually takes these steps:

1.  Arranges with builders to finance the new homeowners' purchases of houses.
2.  Fills out mortgage documents and disburses his own funds to close mortgage loans.
3.  Groups mortgages into a pool or package.
4.  Obtains advance commitments from dealers or investors to buy specified amounts of mortgage-backed securities at set prices and yields.
5.  Requests a commitment to guarantee (form HUD-1704) from GNMA.
6.  Receives a commitment to guarantee from GNMA and is assigned a pool number.
7.  Transfers mortgage documents to a custodial agent.
8.  Submits required documents on the pool to GNMA.
9.  Acquires mortgage-backed Ginnie Mae certificates from GNMA.
10. Delivers Ginnie Mae certificates (the securities) to purchasers (dealers or investors).
11. Is paid by purchasers.
12. After origination has been completed, the originator performs the functions of the issuer, servicing the mortgages in the pool.
13. As issuer, collects all mortgage payments from the various homeowners.
14. Remits monthly payments of principal and interest to investors in the pool and provides each individual certificate holder with a monthly accounting statement (form HUD-1714; illustrated in Section 8.B).

## 2. Pools of Mortgages

Pass-through securities are backed by pools of single-family or multifamily mortgages or by pools of mobile home loans. The majority of certificates issued to date have been backed by pools of new 30-year FHA, FmHA, and VA mortgages on single-family houses.

All of the mortgages in a specific pool are required to be of the same type in terms of interest rate, dwelling class (e.g., single-family, multifamily, etc.), and terms of maturity. The minimum amount of a pool must be $1 million for single-family mortgages and $500,000 for project or mobile home mortgages.

A mortgage banker becomes an issuer when GNMA approves his issuance of securities to be collateralized by a pool of a specified amount of FHA, FmHA, or VA mortgages.

A pool can be terminated at any time prior to the maturity of the outstanding securities, provided that the issuer and all security holders agree to the termination. The issuer may not terminate a pool unilaterally. When formal notification and evidence of mutual agreement are presented, GNMA will cancel its guaranty. All outstanding pool certificates must be returned to GNMA in order to obtain cancellation. Guaranty-fee requirements to GNMA (as described in Section 5.8) cease in the month following the cancellation date.

### 3. Certificates

A Ginnie Mae certificate represents a pro rata share in a pool of FHA-, FmHA-, and/or VA-approved mortgages. Ginnie Mae certificates are issued in registered form in accordance with U.S. Treasury Department regulations. As has been noted, these mortgage-backed certificates are fully and freely transferable and assignable, and thus negotiable securities.

### 4. The Tandem Plan

Under this mortgage assistance program, GNMA commits itself to purchase certain FHA-approved mortgages which are issued by lenders at below-market interest rates. The GNMA purchases are made at prices that provide mortgage holders with incentives to lend at terms favorable to home purchasers with low and moderate incomes. GNMA accumulates these mortgages and periodically auctions them off in packages, either as Ginnie Maes or as whole mortgages.

At times when yields available in the marketplace on

mortgage investments are higher than the rate of interest on the tandem plan mortgages, such loans will sell only at a discount (at less than their face value). Under its tandem plan, GNMA absorbs some of this discount. The tandem plan was developed in 1970 as a form of subsidy to be implemented by GNMA in conjunction with FNMA. An interim selling price (ISP) was established, and GNMA was authorized to implement the program.

Under the tandem plan, GNMA buys the below-market-rate mortgages at prices favorable to originators and in turn favorable to purchasers of new homes. GNMA periodically resells these mortgages to investors at the prevailing market prices and absorbs the difference between the purchase price and the selling price as a subsidy or incentive for new-home construction.

In 1974 an additional version of the plan was initiated for conventional mortgages. Lenders obtain a commitment from FNMA or FHLMC, acting as agents for GNMA, to purchase mortgages with a below-market interest rate, provided that the lower rate is made available to the borrower. When the loans are closed, they are delivered to FNMA or FHLMC, with the discount absorbed by GNMA.

All of these GNMA mortgage purchases are financed by borrowings from the federal government.

Through auctions of single-family or multifamily mortgages, GNMA subsequently sells its purchased mortgages to private investors. Under these procedures GNMA, in effect, operates "in tandem" with private investors to support the nation's building industry by providing below-market-rate loans on terms home buyers can afford.

A typical series of steps initiated by GNMA for the creation and sale of pass-throughs under the tandem plan includes the following:

1. Mortgage bankers originate mortgages and sell them to GNMA at prescribed prices; they are permitted to continue servicing the mortgages.

2. GNMA approaches the mortgage banker to ask him whether he would like to become an issuer of Ginnie Maes.

3. If the mortgage banker accepts, he seeks qualification as an issuer.

4. GNMA notifies a number of mortgage bankers about an upcoming auction with a minimum value of about $150 million.

5. Mortgage bankers send GNMA the required mortgage documents—at this point, GNMA owns the mortgages but the mortgage bankers have the servicing responsibility.

6. GNMA conducts the mortgage auction.

7. The winning bidder pays GNMA in full for the Ginnie Maes.

8. GNMA issues as many certificates (securities) as are needed by the winning syndicate, usually a group of GNMA dealers.

## 5. GNMA Auctions

There are two types of GNMA auctions: securities auctions and whole loan auctions.

Securities auctions were initiated in January 1975. Their basic procedures are:

1. GNMA selects for resale, blocks of mortgages that it has acquired under the tandem plan.

2. The mortgage banker assembles these blocks into pools in preparation for the issuance of mortgage-backed securities.

3. The mortgage banker applies to GNMA for an issuer contract.

4. GNMA arranges for a securities auction.

5. GNMA accepts—on an "all-or-none" basis—bids for pools of the mortgages.

6. GNMA issues to the successful bidding companies or dealer groups as many certificates as are requested and in the denominations specified.

7. The GNMA dealers reoffer the certificates to investors as specified by the terms of the syndicate.

The essential steps in whole mortgage and project mortgage auctions are:

1. GNMA takes bids and offers to sell to mortgage bankers the mortgages it has acquired.
2. The successful bidder may resell the whole mortgages but usually arranges for a takeout for Ginnie Mae securities from GNMA dealers.
3. The winning bidder pays for the mortgages, financing the purchase if necessary, until the GNMA securities can be created and delivered.
4. Mortgage bankers assemble the mortgages into pools.
5. GNMA guarantees the certificates issued under the pools.
6. Mortgage bankers deliver the certificates (securities) to GNMA dealers and/or institutional investors at previously agreed-upon prices.
7. GNMA dealers reoffer the securities to investors.

## C. INTEREST RATES, SERVICING, AND GUARANTEE FEES

The interest rate on a Ginnie Mae security is stated on the face of the certificate. This rate is the interest rate on the FHA, FHDA, and VA mortgages in the pool, less a GNMA guaranty fee of 0.06 percent per annum and the prescribed issuer's servicing fee of 0.44 percent, or a total deduction of 0.50 percent. The price of the security may range above or below par to produce a yield that reflects current market conditions.

Common face interest rates on single-family issues are 9 percent, 8.50 percent, 8.25 percent, 8.00 percent, 7.75 percent, 7.50 percent, 7.25 percent, 7 percent, and 6.50 percent. A few issues are outstanding at other interest rates. See Table 5-1.

**TABLE 5-1**
Ginnie Mae Mortgage-Backed Securities by Interest Rate, September 30, 1977

| Interest Rate | Original Balance (in thousands) | Number of Pools |
|---|---|---|
| 5.50 . . . . . . . . . . . . . . | $   572,631 | 97 |
| 6.50 . . . . . . . . . . . . . . | 5,246,961 | 1,283 |
| 7.00 . . . . . . . . . . . . . . | 570,712 | 162 |
| 7.25 . . . . . . . . . . . . . . | 3,305,455 | 846 |
| 7.50 . . . . . . . . . . . . . . | 9,628,501 | 4,143 |
| 7.75 . . . . . . . . . . . . . . | 499,003 | 184 |
| 8.00 . . . . . . . . . . . . . . | 16,829,976 | 6,978 |
| 8.25 . . . . . . . . . . . . . . | 2,517,863 | 1,212 |
| 8.50 . . . . . . . . . . . . . . | 4,147,480 | 1,935 |
| 9.00 . . . . . . . . . . . . . . | 1,680,800 | 817 |
| 9.50 . . . . . . . . . . . . . . | 167,898 | 180 |
|  | $45,167,280 | 17,837 |
| Various other project and mobile home rates . . . . . . . . | 1,707,526 | 432 |
| Terminated pools . . . . . . . . . | 399,586 | 227 |
| Total Issues . . . . . . . . . . | $47,274,392 | 18,496 |

Source: Government National Mortgage Association.

## D. MATURITY

The stated maturity of a Ginnie Mae depends upon the mortgages that underlie it. Most single-family residential mortgages carry a stated maturity of 30 years.

Although Ginnie Maes are not callable, the mortgages may be prepaid without penalty at any time. Due to the prepayment of principal on single-family and mobile home pools, the expected average life is considerably less than 30 years. The typical market practice is to quote Ginnie Mae yields on a pool of such mortgages to a 12-year half-life (i.e., the point in time when half of the principal amount of the pool is expected to be repaid) (see Section 4.B).

# 6

# Ginnie Mae Markets

## A. INTRODUCTION

The initial offering of Ginnie Maes was sold on February 19, 1970, in the amount of $2 million. Although this first issue was purchased by a pension fund, savings and loan associations and savings banks were quick to note the attractiveness of these new, hybrid instruments—interest-bearing securities with the mortgage feature of self-liquidation. Thrift institutions quickly became major investors in pass-throughs.

As the investment advantages of pass-throughs became better known (e.g., their safety and their competitiveness with alternative vehicles), a broader range of investors became interested. The outstanding face value of Ginnie Maes has grown rapidly among the various types of investors.

This section traces the growth of Ginnie Mae securities and offers some indication of their future potential.

## B. THE PRIMARY MARKET

Primary offerings are purchased from issuers. The volume of such transactions are thought to be directly related to the volume of newly issued securities as tallied by the Government National Mortgage Association each month. Primary transactions can be made on either a cash or a delayed-delivery basis (e.g., immediate settlement or up to six-month delivery).

GNMA statistics on the estimated volume of purchased pass-throughs are based on the original face value of all certificates. Figure 6-1 depicts the growth of new Ginnie Mae

**FIGURE 6-1**
**The Growth in New Issues of Ginnie Mae Securities (in $ millions)**

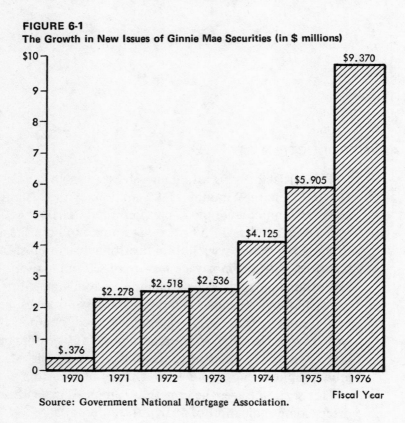

Source: Government National Mortgage Association.

issues since the initial offering in 1970. The annual increases in the outstanding balances of Ginnie Maes over the seven-year period ended June 30, 1976, can be seen in Figure 6-2.

FIGURE 6-2
Outstanding Balances of Ginnie Mae Securities (in $ millions)

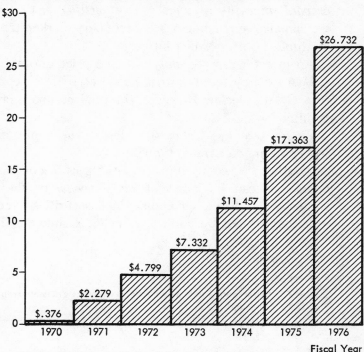

Source: Government National Mortgage Association.

## C. THE SECONDARY MARKET

The expansion in outstanding Ginnie Maes has been aided greatly by an active secondary market and by the market-making capability of the GNMA dealers. Generally, institutional investors prefer to buy and trade securities which enjoy large secondary markets. They tend to avoid "thin" markets in which a large purchase or sale of securities will cause violent price fluctuations. (See Section 4.C for a discussion of the marketability of pass-throughs.)

The secondary market comprises all Ginnie Mae transactions except those done on a primary basis by the issuing mortgage bankers. *The principal amount of a secondary-*

*market transaction will differ from the face amount of the certificate by the amount which has been amortized and prepaid since the issuance of the certificate;* that is, trades are handled on a net basis. Secondary-market transactions are funded with accrued interest.

An investor can generally obtain a price quotation on any GNMA issue by simply providing the certificate's coupon rate to a GNMA dealer. However, the pool number may also be required on old issues.

Figure 6-3 and Table 6-1 depict the rapid growth in secondary-market transactions.

Another index to the expansion of secondary-market operations can be gained from a review of the year-end volume of outstanding Ginnie Mae securities over the six-year span, ended December 31, 1976, as shown in Table 6-2.

**FIGURE 6-3**
**The Increase in Ginnie Mae Secondary-Market Transfers from 1973 through 1976**

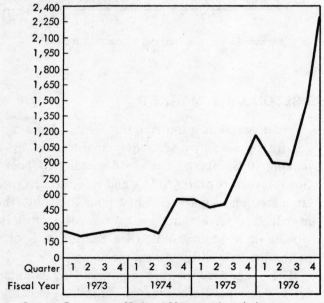

Source: Government National Mortgage Association.

**TABLE 6-1**
**Growth in Ginnie Mae Monthly Secondary-Market Transfers, 1973-1977**
**(in $ millions)**

| Month | 1973 | 1974 | 1975 | 1976 | 1977 |
|-------|------|------|------|------|------|
| January | $ 250 | $ 432 | $ 660 | $ 1,193 | $3,388 |
| February | 283 | 495 | 805 | 1,475 | 3,177 |
| March | 218 | 735 | 1,002 | 1,959 | 4,711 |
| April | 273 | 668 | 1,313 | 2,440 | 3,164 |
| May | 170 | 532 | 972 | 2,513 | 3,732 |
| June | 309 | 529 | 935 | 1,901 | 3,588 |
| July | 396 | 495 | 1,151 | 2,190 | 3,596 |
| August | 303 | 454 | 773 | 2,169 | 3,525 |
| September | 165 | 447 | 817 | 2,783 | |
| October | 218 | 511 | 851 | 2,886 | |
| November | 259 | 429 | 786 | 3,392 | |
| December | 296 | 255 | 1,099 | 4,120 | |
| Total | $3,140 | $6,282 | $11,164 | $29,021 | |

Source: Government National Mortgage Association.

**TABLE 6-2**
**Year-End Volume of Outstanding Ginnie Mae Securities**

| | Year-End Volume of Issued Securities (in $000s) | Percentage Increase over Prior Year |
|---|---|---|
| 1970 | $ 452,034 | – |
| 1971 | 3,154,186 | 568% |
| 1972 | 5,816,077 | 84 |
| 1973 | 8,768,564 | 51 |
| 1974 | 13,321,275 | 52 |
| 1975 | 20,768,541 | 56 |
| 1976 | 34,532,895 | 66 |
| 1977 (September 30) | 47,274,392 | N/A |

Source: Government National Mortgage Association.

Table 6-3 illustrates the growing popularity of mortgage-backed securities among a broader spectrum of investors. The table compares the holdings of the various categories of Ginnie Mae investors at the end of the years 1970, 1973, and 1976.

**TABLE 6-3**
Changes in Distribution of Ginnie Mae Holdings by Type of Investor

|  | Percent of Total | | |
|---|---|---|---|
|  | (At December 31) | | |
|  | 1970 | 1973 | 1976 |
| Savings and loan associations . . . . . . . . . | 53.8% | 33.3% | 19.6% |
| Savings banks . . . . . . . . . . . . . . . . . . | 19.0 | 21.6 | 13.0 |
| Retirement and pension funds . . . . . . . . | 14.9 | 7.0 | 10.0 |
| Commercial banks . . . . . . . . . . . . . . . | 2.2 | 5.7 | 5.4 |
| Credit unions . . . . . . . . . . . . . . . . . . | 1.0 | 5.1 | 2.6 |
| Individuals . . . . . . . . . . . . . . . . . . . | 0.6 | 2.0 | 1.1 |
| Mortgage and investment bankers*† . . . . | 4.1 | 10.0 | 20.3 |
| All others (including nominees)† . . . . . . . | 4.4 | 15.3 | 28.0 |

*Includes securities in transfer and securities held in customer accounts.
†GNMA estimates that in 1976, 13-14 percent in these two categories are owned by pension funds, held in street names and/or the names of nominees.
Note: For later figures see Table 4-2, page 15.
Source: Government National Mortgage Association.

It can be seen from Table 6-3 that over the six-year span 1970-76 the share of Ginnie Maes held by savings and loan associations declined by about two thirds, from 53.8 percent to 19.6 percent. It should also be noted that despite the seeming decline in the share held by retirement and pension funds, security-industry authorities believe that these funds have increased their holdings of Ginnie Maes to a significant degree over the past five years. As indicated in the notes to Table 6-3, GNMA estimates that 13-14 percent in the "Mortgage and investment bankers" and "All others" categories are owned by pension funds.

Despite the considerable expansion in secondary-market transactions revealed by the foregoing statistics, particularly those presented in Table 6-1, these data understate the actual volume of secondary-market transactions. Since GNMA uses its certificate registration records as the basis for its volume statistics, some transactions between dealers and/or investors, as well as many purchases and sales which offset or cancel each other, are not represented in the GNMA figures.

## D. BASES FOR GROWTH EXPECTATIONS

There is ample evidence to support the view that both the primary and secondary Ginnie Mae markets will continue to grow in the years ahead. The reasons for optimism include the following:

1. Housing starts are expected to average over 1.7 million for the years 1976-80.
2. An estimated 1.5 percent annual increase in the adult population through 1985 (as compared to a 1.6 percent annual increase during the 1965-75 period) indicates that new household formation can be expected to continue at a good level.
3. An expected upturn in gross national product is likely to provide the personal income and savings needed to support new-home financing—real GNP is expected to increase at an annual rate of 4.2 percent through 1985, as compared to a 2.6 percent rate of increase for the ten years ending in 1976.
4. Borrowing on mortgages is normally the largest single use of credit in the capital markets.
5. The past successes of mortgage-backed securities in tapping the nation's capital markets portend the expanded use of these securities as an effective tool for the implementation of national housing policy.
6. National housing policy has become a politically acceptable tool used in combating unemployment and achieving various social goals.

# 7

# Ginnie Mae Investors

## A. INTRODUCTION

The number and type of investors in Ginnie Maes have expanded significantly since these instruments were introduced in 1970 (see Section 6). In order to record the market growth of pass-throughs, GNMA has collected data on the outstanding face value of these securities since their inception. The GNMA statistics for the various investor groups will be provided in this section.

The primary purpose of this section is to supplement the general discussion of Ginnie Mae advantages presented in Section 4 and to make that discussion more directly relevant to the needs of specific investor groups. Further details on such subjects as legal eligibility, regulatory requirements, portfolio strategies, and federal tax provisions can be obtained from the trade literature of the various investor categories.

## B. SAVINGS AND LOAN ASSOCIATIONS

### 1. General Characteristics

A savings and loan association is an institution that accepts savings from the public and invests those savings, mainly in mortgage loans. Always a corporation, it may be a mutual institution or, in some states, capital stock association. An association may be either state-chartered or federally chartered. If federally chartered, the word *federal* must be used in the corporate name.

Because of their familiarity with the mortgage-investment field, savings and loans were the first major buyers of Ginnie Maes.

> During the first year [1970] ... the savings and loan industry alone bought over half of the pass-through securities sold. ... Purchasing pass-through securities offers the manager of a savings and loan association real incentives to enter the government-insured mortgage market because the cost of this form of entry is much cheaper than direct participation. First, an association does not need to recruit originators and mortgage processing personnel familiar with FHA/VA procedures. Second, since only one piece of paper is purchased, and since GNMA supervises the issuer to insure quality performance, it is not necessary to have personnel review both the myriad of paperwork accompanying the usual mortgage instrument and the originator-servicer's performance.[1]

The alternative forms of real estate mortgage investments available to savings and loan associations to finance housing include:

1. Local home mortgage loans.
2. Purchase of out-of-state mortgages from others.
3. Purchase of participations in loans originated by others.

---

[1] Phillip C. Kidd, "One Year Old and Going Strong!" *Mortgage Banker*, May 1971.

4. Buying Ginnie Maes or other mortgage-backed securities.[2]
5. Providing construction funds for builders/developers.

A statement of the condition of all savings and loans as of December 31, 1976, indicated that 82.4 percent of their total assets was invested in "mortgage loans outstanding" and that 85.7 percent of their total liabilities and net worth was represented by savings deposits. Additional perspective on the role of savings and loans in the mortgage field can be obtained from Table 7-1.

**TABLE 7-1**
**Mortgage Loans Outstanding, by Type of Lender, Year-End 1976 (preliminary)**

| Lender | $ Billions | Percent |
|---|---|---|
| Savings and loan associations | 323.1 | 36.5% |
| Commercial banks | 147.7 | 16.7 |
| Savings banks (mutual) | 81.5 | 9.2 |
| Life insurance companies | 91.5 | 10.3 |
| All others | 242.3 | 27.3 |
| Total | 886.1 | 100.0% |

Source: United States League of Savings Associations, *Savings and Loan Fact Book,* 1976.

## 2. Investment in Ginnie Maes

As of December 31, 1976, the face value of Ginnie Maes held by savings and loan associations totaled $6.8 billion. Of the eight Ginnie Mae investor groups identified by GNMA, savings and loan associations held the largest share—19.6 percent—of the total amount invested in pass-throughs.

## 3. Special Considerations for Savings and Loan Associations

1. Savings and loan associations may make investments in Ginnie Maes (12 Code of Federal Regulations 545.9c),

---

*Such as participation certificates issued by the Federal Home Loan Mortgage Corporation (Freddy Mac PCs).

though they may not include these investments as "liquid assets" for purposes of meeting the requirements adopted by the Federal Home Loan Bank Board.

2. Ginnie Mae investments made by savings and loan associations are not subject to any percentage of assets or area limitations normally applicable to the loans of these organizations.

3. For purposes of determining the amount of capital stock that member savings and loan associations are required to hold in their district Federal Home Loan Bank, mortgage-backed securities based on loans to finance single-family, multifamily, and apartment-type dwellings are all considered to be "home mortgage loans."

4. Savings and loan associations which are located in capital-surplus areas or are faced with excess liquid assets held at low yield can buy and sell Ginnie Maes in the same way as they can buy and sell any other negotiable security.

5. During periods of unexpected or extraordinarily high deposit inflows, Ginnie Maes provide savings and loan associations with an immediate alternative to investments in nonmortgage assets or low-yield short-term vehicles.

## 4. Bookkeeping

The simplicity of bookkeeping for Ginnie Maes is discussed in Section 8.J. Of considerable interest to small savings and loan associations is the single monthly check for principal and interest due on each certificate held.

Premiums and discounts involved in the purchase of GNMA securities can be amortized over a period of years as discussed below. Profits and losses on the sale of GNMA securities are generally credited to or charged against current income.

## 5. Federal Tax Provisions

Ginnie Maes are considered assets as described in Section 7701(a)(19)(c) of the Internal Revenue Code for purposes of meeting the percentage of total assets requirements of "domestic building and loan associations." In addition, Ginnie Maes may be treated as "qualifying real property loans" (Section 593[e] of the Code), against which a savings and loan association can take a deduction on its tax return for an allocation to its bad debt reserve.

The question of how to amortize discounts and premiums properly on Ginnie Maes has not yet been fully answered. There is still some disagreement as to whether savings and loan associations should treat Ginnie Maes as investment securities or as mortgage loans. Whether premiums and discounts should be amortized over the average life, the full term to maturity, or some other estimated life will be determined by savings and loan regulations, the IRS Code, and independent accounting counsel.

Some savings and loan supervisory authorities have ruled that Ginnie Maes are to be treated in the same way as "other investment securities." This means that discounts and premiums are amortized over the remaining life of the security rather than during the shorter period authorized for loans under FSLIC regulation 563.231. Either straight-line or level-interest amortization may be used.

The IRS regards Ginnie Maes as mortgage loans in this context. For this reason, many investors choose to amortize premiums on Ginnie Maes over the life of the loan. Typically, however, Ginnie Mae securities pay off earlier than their stated maturities, and to the extent that they do, the premium or discount may be amortized in accordance with the liquidation of the principal.

## C. SAVINGS BANKS

### 1. General Characteristics

As thrift institutions, savings banks meet their obligations to their depositors by safeguarding principal, providing a moderate return on savings, and permitting immediate withdrawal of deposits. Most savings banks are of the "mutual" type; that is, they are owned by their depositors and are operated by trustees for the depositors' benefit.

Mutual savings banks are chartered in 17 states and Puerto Rico. Most of the states in which these banks are chartered have enacted legislation regulating their investments. The following regulations are typical:

1. Up to 65 percent of total mutual savings bank assets can be invested in mortgages and real estate.
2. Generally acceptable investments by mutual savings banks include investments in U.S. Treasuries, federal agency obligations, municipal bonds, and corporate bonds (utility, industrial, and railroad). All investments must meet either the approval of state boards or certain minimum credit specifications.

To enable savings banks to meet their objectives of protecting their depositors' principal, furnishing depositors with a return, and allowing depositors to make immediate withdrawals, the investments of savings banks must be prudent and marketable and must generate an adequate yield.

Savings banks and savings and loan associations (both of which are "thrift institutions") have a great deal in common. Consequently, much of what was said in Section 7.B about savings and loan associations will be equally applicable to savings banks.

## 2. Investment in Ginnie Maes

As of December 31, 1976, savings banks held $4.5 billion in Ginnie Mae securities. Their 13 percent share of total Ginnie Mae holdings put them in fourth place among the eight types of investors recorded by GNMA (see Table 6.3).

## 3. Special Considerations for Savings Banks

It should be remembered that savings banks have broader investment authority than do their savings and loan counterparts. For savings banks the Ginnie Mae is an alternative to other types of investments. Therefore, savings banks must compare the relative yield on Ginnie Maes with a more broadly defined base than that used by savings and loan associations, including corporate bonds.

Savings banks have had long experience with investments in self-originated and FHA and VA mortgages, both locally and through their correspondent systems. Ginnie Maes offer savings banks yields comparable to those obtainable on self-originated mortgages as well as the previously cited advantages of marketability, administrative simplicity, and diversification (see Section 4).

Another factor which savings banks should weigh carefully is that eligible mortgage originations can be pooled for inclusion in pass-throughs. This permits these loans to acquire attributes of marketability not normally ascribed to whole loans. The availability of the pooling procedure gives savings banks the option of retaining an investment or of selling it in either pooled or whole-loan form.

In either case, savings banks also have the option of retaining or selling the servicing function. It must be stressed, however, that unless the pooling decision is made in the first year of a mortgage, these options become inoperative.

Ginnie Mae securities can be bought and sold with relative ease. After a few phone calls to get the level of market prices, a transaction can be closed quickly. This contrasts sharply with the reviews of individual loan files, the inspection trips, and the customized funding requirements that are necessary when savings banks purchase a group of individual mortgages. Supervision of the mortgage servicer is also eliminated.

## 4. Bookkeeping

The comments in Section 7.B.4 are for the most part applicable to savings banks.

Field research for this manual indicated that savings banks required only their regular staff of people to maintain all the essential bookkeeping records for their Ginnie Mae holdings.

### 5. Federal Tax Provisions

Internal Revenue Service rulings 70-544 and 70-545 regard Ginnie Maes as qualified assets for favorable tax treatment.

Savings banks can also benefit from several of the income tax advantages discussed in connection with savings and loan associations in Section 7.B.5.

## D. RETIREMENT AND PENSION FUNDS

### 1. General Characteristics

Public and private funds have been created by employers to provide retirement benefits for employees. A wide range of conditions exist in these funds: employer and/or employee contributions, differences in retirement age, and variations in vesting rights. The funds are usually directed by a board of trustees and are established in accordance with federal and state regulations.

Retirement and pension fund trustees perform the twofold fiduciary function of protecting their assets for future beneficiaries while simultaneously obtaining optimum yield. Some funds are self-administered by an in-house investment staff, whereas others are managed by such outside professional specialists as investment counselors and bank trust personnel.

The GNMA category of retirement and pension funds includes endowment funds, health and welfare trusts, union trust funds, and public funds. In the interest of simplicity, this manual designates all investors included in GNMA's retirement and pension funds category as "pension funds."

Private pension funds have not been traditional mortgage buyers. Some public pension fund managers have acquired the technical knowledge needed to cope successfully with the intricacies of direct investments in mortgages.

These funds represented a prime target during the conceptualization and design of the Ginnie Mae security. Through the Ginnie Mae, the designers of mortgage-backed securities sought to achieve two basic objectives: (1) to channel the dramatically expanding pension fund assets into the housing market; and (2) to promote the social benefits to be derived from financing low- and moderate-cost housing.

As has already been noted, John Evans, former director of the AFL-CIO department of urban affairs, urged the pension funds, which he termed "a $370 billion giant," to invest more of their assets in mortgages in order to help the nation meet its housing needs. Ginnie Maes permit pension funds to invest in mortgage-backed vehicles without becoming involved in mortgage-related paperwork and technical details.

## 2. Investment in Ginnie Maes

On December 31, 1976, pension funds ranked fifth among the eight investor classes established by GNMA (see Table 6.3). At that time, according to the GNMA figures, the original face value of pension fund investments in passthroughs was $3.5 billion. Some trade sources believe that the inclusion of Ginnie Maes owned by retirement and pension funds but held in street names and the names of nominees would raise this amount to between $5 billion and $8 billion.

Despite the tailoring of Ginnie Maes to suit their portfolio requirements, most pension fund managers have been slow to recognize the advantages of these securities. Where there has been acceptance, however, it has been overwhelming.

## 3. Considerations for Retirement and Pension Funds

The U.S. government guaranty makes mortgage-backed pass-throughs eligible investments for public and other regulated pension funds. The safety of Ginnie Maes has the key advantage of enabling pension fund managers to meet their first major fiduciary responsibility—safeguarding investments to fulfill the vested rights of retirees.

Obtaining an attractive yield is the second major fiduciary responsibility of pension fund managers. When the full faith and credit guaranty of Ginnie Maes are considered, it becomes apparent that they offer a viable alternative to competitive capital-market instruments.

Pass-throughs enable pension fund fiduciaries to comply with at least two provisions of the recently enacted Employment Retirement Income Security Act of 1974 (ERISA). This law "requires that fiduciaries of a pension plan diversify assets to minimize the risk of large losses, unless it is clearly not prudent to do so." The full faith and credit guaranty gives the investor the highest credit status available, thus relieving the manager of most of the responsibility for achieving adequate portfolio diversification.

ERISA also specified an annual appraisal of each fund's asset value. An active secondary market in Ginnie Maes provides readily available market quotations. This contrasts markedly with the difficulties encountered by funds in valuing some other bond and equity-type securities.

The continuous cash flow feature of pass-throughs (see Section 4.E) should be particularly interesting to pension funds since the actuarially determined payment needs of pension funds require a predictable flow of income to meet ongoing cash disbursements. Portfolio holdings of Ginnie Maes obviate the necessity of selling other securities in fluctuating markets to generate needed cash.

Moreover, mortgage-backed instruments permit pension fund managers to think in terms of community benefits as well as their responsibilities to retirees. (In this connection, it might be noted that the establishment of pension funds is itself a recognition of social responsibility.) Many administrators of state pension programs feel that they have an implied obligation to support their local mortgage markets. From time to time, various governmental bodies have indicated a preference for policies that favor increased investment by pension funds in mortgage-related vehicles connected with local or regional housing. Ginnie Maes allow fiduciaries to invest in such mortgages since the liquidity of pass-throughs is assured through their marketability.

Unions, particularly in the construction trades, might demonstrate a certain degree of self interest by mandating that a specified percentage of the assets in their pension funds go into mortgage-backed instruments. These and similar pension funds might discover an additional advantage of Ginnie Maes—they can be used to help their own participants finance their homes while providing the investment attributes of safety and an attractive yield.

## 4. Bookkeeping

The paperwork involved in purchasing and selling pass-throughs and in maintaining the necessary monthly accounting records is quite simple. There is no need for in-depth knowledge of real estate principles or mortgage documentation procedures. Mortgage-backed Ginnie Maes can be handled as easily as any other actively traded securities (see Section 8.J).

Compliance with ERISA regulations is facilitated by the "Issuer's Monthly Remittance Advice" (form HUD-1714, shown in Section 8.B). This document, which is distributed to each certificate holder with a check on the 15th day of each month, lists the net outstanding balance of principal. Thus, the net asset value of pass-through holdings can be readily ascertained.

## 5. Federal Tax Provision

According to IRS Ruling 70-545, the purchase of Ginnie Maes does not impair the tax-exempt status of a pension fund in any way.

## E. COMMERCIAL BANKS

### 1. General Characteristics

A commercial bank is a lending institution that takes in *demand deposits,* as well as time deposits accepted by a savings bank or a savings and loan association. A commercial bank offers a wide variety of loans and credit instruments to business and industry. Although there are minor technical differences between national (federal) and state banks, in the interest of simplicity this manual treats all commercial banks as a single class.

Only the portfolio or dealer Ginnie Mae transactions of commercial banks are included here. In accordance with GNMA practice, the trust department transactions of commercial banks are included in the "Retirement and Pension Fund" category.

Depending upon the probable future behavior of a commercial bank's deposits and upon the nature of its assets, the bank's management sets levels for cash and for secondary reserves, the latter being based primarily on short-term securities. Because of the safety, marketability, and legal eligibility of government securities, commercial banks favor the use of these securities as secondary reserves.

To earn optimum profits, commercial banks must balance four functions: (1) managing cash to meet demand requirements; (2) obtaining legally eligible assets with maximum yield to collateralize public funds; (3) generating the best overall return while performing the cyclical "balance wheel" operation of buying marketable securities as loan demand decreases and selling securities as loan demand accelerates; and (4) creating a stable source of income from assets.

From an operational stance, a commercial bank can be considered "liability-managed" or "asset-managed." A liability-managed bank is usually a large money-market institution with sufficient creditworthiness to raise funds in the open market. An asset-managed bank is normally a smaller institution which does not finance its business through certificates of deposit.

## 2. Investments in Ginnie Maes

On December 31, 1976, according to the GNMA statistics, commercial bank holdings of pass-throughs amounted to $1.9 billion, or 5.4 percent of all outstanding securities. This was equal to about one third of the Ginnie Mae holdings of savings banks—an understandable relationship since savings banks have been traditionally heavy investors in mortgages and mortgage-related vehicles.

In all likelihood, the commercial bank holdings of Ginnie Maes are understated since the GNMA statistics do not include the face value of certificates held in the names of nominees. (The GNMA statistics are based on the registered names of certificate holders.)

## 3. Special Considerations for Commercial Banks

*a. For "Liability-Managed" Commercial Banks.* These institutions have developed an increased interest in the use of pass-throughs as a means of performing their balance wheel function. This function involves the ever-shifting relationship between the loans and the securities assets of commercial banks. As loan demand increases, commercial banks generally reduce their investments in short-term securities to generate more cash. Conversely, as loan demand decreases and cash on hand builds up, commercial banks reduce their cash surplus by making investments in short-term vehicles.

Here, in simplified form, are some of the general methods by which liability-managed banks take advantage of the investment attributes of Ginnie Maes:

1. Improve overall yields by purchasing liquid short-term instruments. At the top, or heavy, phase of the loan cycle, when outstanding loans start to liquidate, begin buying pass-throughs for their relatively attractive yields.

2. Obtain a favorable yield spread—issue certificates of deposit and invest the proceeds in Ginnie Maes. Note, however, the obvious pitfalls inherent in borrowing short term to invest long term.

3. Benefit from the marginal cost differential between liquid funds and noncurrent assets—seize favorable opportunities to trade off holdings of CDs, federal funds, and similar vehicles against pass-throughs.

4. Lower the bank's effective income tax rate—banks which generate foreign tax credits and other tax reductions from such activities as leasing can use purchases of non-interest-exempt securities (including Ginnie Maes) as income tax offsets.

5. Obtain a maximum return on the stable portion of public funds collateral. Some types of public funds—state tax receipts, for example—fluctuate widely on a seasonal basis. However, statistical studies often disclose that a "stable and predictable" amount of collateral is required throughout the year for the various public funds of a bank's clients. This stable and predictable amount can be invested in such government-guaranteed securities as Ginnie Maes at a higher yield than that available from other types of collateral authorized for public funds.

6. Buy Ginnie Maes for delayed delivery. When a sector of a bank's funds develops a negative spread (that is, the cost of the money to the bank is greater than the return on the money), the bank can use the delayed-delivery market to counterbalance anticipated changes in its loan demand and its assets.

7. Use pass-throughs for arbitrage transactions—that is, use the long side of pass-throughs as collateral for borrowing on the short position (the safety of Ginnie Maes permits their ready acceptance as collateral by the lending institution). Here the short side takes advantage of the delayed-delivery capability of these securities, thus offsetting the mechanical problem of borrowing instruments to effect delivery.

*b. For "Asset-Managed" Commercial Banks.* These institutions generally do not have the same investment flexibility as liability-managed banks since they generally do not use the certificate of deposit market as a source of funds. Many asset-managed banks can adapt the above types of transactions to their own operations, depending upon the size of their assets, the regulatory climate, and management policies.

*c. Legal Eligibility.* On April 16, 1970, in a letter to Woodward Kingman, president of GNMA, the Comptroller of the Currency ruled:

1. National banks may purchase mortgage-backed securities for investments without limitation as to amount.
2. National banks may purchase mortgage-backed securities in their fiduciary capacity.
3. Since mortgage-backed securities are fully guaranteed by GNMA, they are exempt from the limitations contained in Paragraph 7 of 12 USC 24, from the registration requirements pursuant to Section 3(a)(2) of the Securities Act of 1933, and from Part 16 of the regulations of the Comptroller of the Currency (12 CFR 16).

Opinions have been received from most state regulatory authorities that state-chartered banks under their jurisdiction may invest in GNMA mortgage-backed securities. These opinions are available in the Washington, D.C., offices of GNMA. See Table 4-3 for a state-by-state overview.

## 4. Bookkeeping

Most commercial banks must comply with record-keeping procedures prescribed by state or federal authorities. Bookkeeping for pass-throughs can be handled with the comparative ease of bookkeeping for any other negotiable security.

## 5. Federal Tax Provisions

Commercial banks do not gain any special tax advantages from their purchases or sales of Ginnie Maes. The interest these banks receive on Ginnie Maes is treated as ordinary income, and monthly payments of principal are considered a return of capital.

## F. CREDIT UNIONS

### 1. General Characteristics

A credit union consists of a group of members who own and operate their organization on a cooperative basis. The members elect the directors and supervisory personnel. A credit union grants loans to its members at relatively low interest rates. For example, most credit unions limit their interest rates on loans to a maximum of 12 percent annually. Being nonprofit financial cooperatives, credit unions usually pay their members comparatively high interest rates on their savings.

In contrast to savings and loan associations, which usually confine their lending to home building, credit unions grant loans primarily for such personal needs as buying automobiles and financing vacations.

As compared to banks, credit unions do not require heavy capitalization. They may be chartered under state laws or through the National Credit Union Administration. Preliminary 1976 year-end figures showed that 34 million people in the United States were members of 22,608 credit unions with total assets of over $39 billion.[3]

Although credit unions are reportedly the fastest-growing financial institutions in the nation, they are still relatively small compared with commercial banks, savings and loan associations, and mutual savings banks (see Table 7-2).

At the close of 1976, credit unions were classified as shown in Table 7-3.

By pooling their resources through central credit unions, individual credit unions obtain economies of size which pro-

---

[3] Credit Union National Association, *Yearbook: 1977.*

**TABLE 7-2**
**Savings Accounts in Major Types of Banking Institutions, December 31, 1976**

| Type of Institution | Savings (in $ billions) |
|---|---|
| Commercial banks | $487.9 |
| Savings and loan associations | 336.0 |
| Mutual savings banks | 122.0 |
| Credit unions | 44.8 |

Source: Credit Union National Association, *Yearbook: 1977*.

**TABLE 7-3**
**Credit Unions by Type, December 31, 1976**

| Category | Percentage of Total |
|---|---|
| Occupational | 55.9% |
| Associational | 17.0 |
| Federal, state, county, and local government | 15.5 |
| Educational services | 8.0 |
| Residential | 3.6 |

Source: Credit Union National Association, *Yearbook: 1977*.

vide improved efficiency, lower costs, better investment returns, and more recognition in the financial marketplace. The overall credit union structure embraces the following segments:

1. Credit unions—governed by a board of directors elected by the members.
2. Chapters—formed by credit unions to provide helpful programs within a region.
3. Leagues—operated by directors elected from member credit unions, often on a statewide basis. Supported by dues from member credit unions.
4. Credit Union National Association—managed by nationwide directors elected by member leagues. Funded by dues from leagues and from credit unions in nonleague areas.
5. World Council of Credit Unions—directed by a board and

delegates named by national and regional confederations and free-standing leagues, and financed by the dues of these confederations and leagues.

## 2. Investments in Ginnie Maes

On December 31, 1976, credit union holdings of pass-throughs amounted to $9 million, or 2.6 percent of the face value of all outstanding Ginnie Maes. These holdings placed credit unions seventh among GNMA's eight investor categories.

Federally chartered credit unions are authorized to buy pass-throughs by Section 8(8) of the Federal Credit Union Act (12 U.S. Code 1757). The legal eligibility of mortgage-backed securities as portfolio holdings for state-chartered credit unions is determined by the respective state authorities (see the "Credit Unions" column of Table 4-3).

## 3. Special Considerations for Credit Unions

The typical credit union is faced with the investment problem of coping with its members' needs for both short-term (demand) and long-term savings plans. When demand deposits rise above a certain level, experience indicates that a specific percentage of these deposit liabilities can be utilized to acquire income-producing assets with longer maturity dates.

Occasionally, longer-term investors in credit unions will withdraw some of their funds for redeposit in other money-market institutions or instruments as opportunities for better yields present themselves. Thus, the investment policies of credit unions must be such that the portfolio managers can sell some of their longer-term investments rapidly to generate cash for withdrawal demands. As has been pointed out in Section 4.C, the large secondary market in Ginnie Maes and the ready negotiability of these vehicles provide a quick route to needed cash.

## 4. Bookkeeping

Many credit unions have extremely small staffs and cannot afford elaborate administrative procedures to control their internal operations. For such credit unions, the bookkeeping advantages of pass-throughs should be of particular interest. Pass-throughs are comparatively simple to manage; no knowledge of real estate procedures is required to handle them; and record keeping is minimal. Being negotiable instruments, Ginnie Maes can be handled as easily as any comparable government security or any high-grade corporate obligation.

## 5. Federal Tax Provision

Federal credit unions are totally exempt from all federal, state, and local taxation, except property levies. Their tax-exempt status is based on Paragraph 23 of the Federal Credit Union Act of 1934. Most state-chartered credit unions are also exempt from federal income taxes.

## G. INDIVIDUALS

### 1. General Characteristics

The following material should not be regarded as investment, legal, or tax advice. Its sole purpose is to present a brief analysis of individual investors as a class under GNMA's statistical structure.

The investment goals of individuals vary widely, so only very general comments can be made here. Many individuals, particularly those near retirement, require safety, diversification, relative price stability, marketability, and a good yield as criteria for their investments. Accordingly, such individuals frequently prefer government securities for at least some portion of their portfolios.

Ginnie Maes should be of interest to buyers of government securities, mortgages, and annuities. Their unique advantages of safety, attractive yield, marketability, administrative simplicity, continuous cash flow, and diversification offer sound appeal for many individuals.

However, the individual investor should bear in mind that because of the return of principal through amortization and prepayments—the self-liquidating feature of Ginnie Maes—the entire amount of the principal will have been received by maturity.

## 2. Investment in Ginnie Maes

As of December 31, 1976, individual owners of these securities represented the smallest of the segments monitored by GNMA—$345 million, or 1.1 percent of all outstanding Ginnie Mae issues.

Three types of investments by individuals in Ginnie Maes are:

1. *Trusts.* Ginnie Maes are suitable for living or testamentary trusts. They also can be used for such special-purpose funds as alimony-payment reserves, gifts to minors, and for monthly retirement income.

2. *Single-payment annuity.* Ginnie Maes are becoming increasingly popular as retirement-income funds. A person aged 60, for example, could buy one or more Ginnie Maes and thus probably receive a higher return per year than would be obtainable from an annuity of the same amount. Moreover, in addition to offering the highest degree of safety, Ginnie Maes, unlike annuities, are negotiable and can be resold in the secondary market.

3. *Installment sale.* One illustration of this type of investment would be the sale of an appreciated low-tax-basis security by a father to a grown son, payable over a period of years. The son immediately sells the security and reinvests the proceeds, using the income from the new investment to pay out the father. The father elects to report his capital gain

on the installment plan, thereby both lowering and deferring his capital gains tax. The IRS requires an interest rate of at least 4 percent on the unpaid installments. The yield from Ginnie Maes can be used by the son to comfortably provide for this 4 percent interest requirement.

A normal round lot of Ginnie Maes is $1 million. But some dealers will sell blocks down to $100,000 at competitive prices. The smallest face value of these instruments is $25,000 (original balance) and the values of certificates increase in $5,000 increments thereafter.

## 3. Special Considerations for Individuals

Many retired people find two benefits in Ginnie Maes as compared with other securities:

1. The highest degree of safety, based on the full faith and credit of the United States.
2. Regular monthly checks instead of the semiannual interest payments on corporate bonds.

## 4. Bookkeeping

Certificate holders receive an "Issuer's Monthly Remittance Advice" (form HUD-1714) along with their monthly checks. This document shows the respective amounts of the cash distribution applicable to principal amortization and to interest. Figure 8-1 reproduces this form.

## 5. Federal Tax Provisions

Interest that individual investors receive on Ginnie Maes is generally regarded as ordinary income. Monthly payments of principal are normally treated as a return of capital. The sale of Ginnie Mae securities by individuals involves capital gains or losses for short-term or long-term capital gains treatment.

# 8

# Administrative
# Clearance Procedures

## A. BUYING AND SELLING FOR IMMEDIATE DELIVERY

The immediate or cash market for Ginnie Maes is considered to be for settlement within the calendar month. This is the most common buying transaction used by portfolio managers. "Immediates" (usually offered by dealers rather than issuers) constitute an opportunity to invest monies without having to make an interim short-term investment of the funds.

The immediate market offers the investor a traditional means to liquidate securities which have been held in portfolio, as well as a market in which delayed-delivery positions can be sold prior to delivery, as they become "immediates." This latter move has been widely employed to take cash profits by investors who purchased securities for delayed delivery and found themselves with a gain that could be booked as current income.

Ginnie Mae securities are usually priced in increments of 1/32d of 1 percent of par. Certificates for single-family pools are quoted on the basis of prepayment in 12 years (sometimes referred to as 12-year average life or 12-year half-life).

## B. PRINCIPAL AND INTEREST REMITTANCE

Monthly payments are made to registered Ginnie Mae certificate holders by the issuer no later than the 15th calendar day of the month following that in which collections on the pooled mortgages were made. Each payment is accompanied by an "Issuer's Monthly Remittance Advice" (form HUD-1714) (see Figure 8-1).

The record date for the certificate is the last business day of the month. Scheduled payments of principal and interest are not necessarily uniform over the life of the certificate. Monthly payments may be supplemented from time to time by prepayment of mortgages in the pool. Prepayments are distributed on a pro rata basis to all registered certificate holders.

A completed "Issuer's Monthly Remittance Advice" contains the following information:

1. Security holder: Name of registered owner.
2. GNMA pool number: For which payment is being made.
3. Certificate number: For which payment is being made.
4. Security interest rate: Annual interest rate of certificate.
5. Date: Issuance date of the "advice."
6. Reporting month: For which the principal and interest are being paid.
7. Pro rata share percentage: Percentage of the total pool that this certificate represents.
8. Details: A through E detail the principal (C includes any prepayment), adjustments, and total cash distribution.
9. Outstanding balance: New balance of the certificate after this remittance is paid.
10. Issuer: Name, address, and signature of the mortgage banker servicing this pool.

**FIGURE 8-1**

| U. S. DEPARTMENT OF HOUSING AND URBAN DEVELOPMENT |
| --- |

U. S. DEPARTMENT OF HOUSING AND URBAN DEVELOPMENT<br>
GOVERNMENT NATIONAL MORTGAGE ASSOCIATION<br>
MORTGAGE-BACKED SECURITIES PROGRAM<br>
ISSUER'S MONTHLY REMITTANCE ADVICE

TO THE FOLLOWING SECURITY HOLDER:

| GNMA POOL NUMBER | DATE |
| --- | --- |
| CERTIFICATE NUMBER | REPORTING MONTH |
| SECURITY INTEREST RATE | PRO RATA SHARE PERCENTAGE |

This remittance advice covers the above security holder's proportional share of the distribution in the indicated pool of mortgages for the above reporting month. ☐ The check is enclosed. ☐ The check will be forwarded separately but no later than the 15th of the current month.

| | | |
| --- | --- | --- |
| A. | Cash distribution due holder for scheduled principal amortization | $ |
| B. | Cash distribution due holder for interest | |
| C. | Cash distribution of additional principal collections | |
| D. | Adjustments (+ or −) *(Explain)* | |
| E. | Total cash distribution due holder | $ |
| F. | Outstanding balance of this certificate after credit of above distribution | $ |

EXPLANATION FOR ITEM D:

I hereby certify that the information contained herein is true to the best of my knowledge and belief.

| | |
| --- | --- |
| *(Issuer)* | *(Authorized Signature)* |
| *(Street Address)* | *(City and State)* |

*In the event of transfer of the security, the most recent Remittance Advice must accompany the certificate.*

## C. THE CERTIFICATE

A properly issued certificate (Figure 8-2) contains the following information:

1. Registered owner: Name of registered owner.
2. Original principal amount: Value of certificate.
3. Certificate number: Assigned by GNMA; "SF" denotes single-family mortgage pool.
4. Indenture: Term of loan or bond agreement.
5. Date of issue: Issuance date for the total pool.
6. Single-family mortgage pool number: Assigned by GNMA to issuer.
7. Interest rate: Annual interest rate of certificate.
8. Initial payment date: Date on which first monthly remittance of principal and interest is due.
9. Original principal amount: Same amount as 2.
10. Original aggregate amount of pool: Original amount of total pool.
11. Maturity date: Due date for final payment of pool.
12. Transfer date: Effective transfer date on books of GNMA and issuer.
13. Issuer: Name of mortgage banker servicing pool.

The back, or assignment, section of a certificate is filled out as follows:

1. Assignee: Fill in name of assignee (a) when transferring certificate; (b) when it is desirable to render the certificate nonnegotiable (e.g., for safety during mail delivery). Do not fill in when certificate is being transferred to a street name.
2. Signature of assignor: Registered owner must sign manually to effect transfer or delivery of certificate. When 3 and 4 are filled in, a signature on this line makes the certificate fully negotiable.
3. Signature of witnessing officer: Witness to assignor's signature must sign here. The reverse side of "Special Form of Detached Assignment for United States Regis-

**FIGURE 8-2**

68

**FIGURE 8-2** *(continued)*

## ASSIGNMENT

I AM THE OWNER, OR THE DULY AUTHORIZED REPRESENTATIVE OF THE OWNER, OF THE WITHIN MORTGAGE BACKED CERTIFICATE AND FOR VALUE RECEIVED HEREBY ASSIGN THE SAME TO

(1)

_____
(ASSIGNEE)
AND AUTHORIZE THE TRANSFER THEREOF ON THE BOOKS OF THE ISSUER.

(2)

_____
(SIGNATURE OF ASSIGNOR)
PERSONALLY APPEARED BEFORE ME THE ABOVE NAMED PERSON, WHOSE IDENTITY IS WELL KNOWN OR PROVED TO ME, AND SIGNED THE ABOVE ASSIGNMENT, ACKNOWLEDGING IT TO BE HIS FREE ACT AND DEED. WITNESS MY HAND, OFFICIAL DESIGNATION, AND SEAL.

(3)

_____        _____
(SIGNATURE OF WITNESSING OFFICER)              (OFFICIAL DESIGNATION)

(4)

SEAL    DATED AT_____    _____, 19___

## ASSIGNMENT

I AM THE OWNER, OR THE DULY AUTHORIZED REPRESENTATIVE OF THE OWNER, OF THE WITHIN MORTGAGE BACKED CERTIFICATE AND FOR VALUE RECEIVED HEREBY ASSIGN THE SAME TO

(5)

_____
(ASSIGNEE)
AND AUTHORIZE THE TRANSFER THEREOF ON THE BOOKS OF THE ISSUER.

(6)

_____
(SIGNATURE OF ASSIGNOR)
PERSONALLY APPEARED BEFORE ME THE ABOVE NAMED PERSON, WHOSE IDENTITY IS WELL KNOWN OR PROVED TO ME, AND SIGNED THE ABOVE ASSIGNMENT, ACKNOWLEDGING IT TO BE HIS FREE ACT AND DEED. WITNESS MY HAND, OFFICIAL DESIGNATION, AND SEAL.

(7)

_____        _____
(SIGNATURE OF WITNESSING OFFICER)              (OFFICIAL DESIGNATION)

(8)

SEAL    DATED AT_____    _____, 19___

SPECIMEN

## INSTRUCTIONS

TO ASSIGN THIS MORTGAGE BACKED CERTIFICATE, THE OWNER, OR HIS DULY AUTHORIZED REPRESENTATIVE, SHALL APPEAR BEFORE AN OFFICER AUTHORIZED TO WITNESS ASSIGNMENTS, ESTABLISH HIS IDENTITY TO THE SATISFACTION OF SUCH OFFICER, AND IN HIS PRESENCE EXECUTE THE ASSIGNMENT, USING ONE OF THE ABOVE FORMS. THE WITNESSING OFFICER MUST THEN AFFIX HIS SIGNATURE, OFFICIAL DESIGNATION, AND SEAL, IF ANY, AND ADD THE PLACE AND DATE OF EXECUTION. OFFICERS AUTHORIZED TO WITNESS ASSIGNMENTS INCLUDE EXECUTIVE OFFICERS OF BANKS AND TRUST COMPANIES INCORPORATED IN THE UNITED STATES OR ITS ORGANIZED TERRITORIES, AND THEIR BRANCHES, DOMESTIC AND FOREIGN. IF ADDITIONAL ASSIGNMENTS ARE REQUIRED, A FORM SIMILAR TO THE ABOVE MAY BE WRITTEN OR TYPED HEREON. FULL INFORMATION REGARDING ASSIGNMENTS MAY BE OBTAINED FROM GOVERNMENT NATIONAL MORTGAGE ASSOCIATION.

### IMPORTANT

THE PRESENT PRINCIPAL BALANCE OF THIS MORTGAGE BACKED CERTIFICATE IS NOT NECESSARILY THE ORIGINAL PRINCIPAL AMOUNT SHOWN ON ITS FACE. THE PRESENT PRINCIPAL BALANCE OF THE CERTIFICATE MAY BE ASCERTAINED FROM THE ISSUER NAMED THEREON OR A DEALER IN SUCH SECURITIES.

tered Securities" (Department of the Treasury form PD 1832) cites officers authorized to certify assignments (see Figure 8-4).

4. Seal: Raised seal of the witnessing bank must be affixed here. Location and date of assignment must also be indicated.

5-8. Assignment: An additional assignment may be made only after the prior assignment has been completed.

## D. THE BALANCE OF A CERTIFICATE

The outstanding balance of any certificate may be obtained by referring to monthly factor books (Figure 8-3) which are published by both The Bond Buyer (as the "Government National Mortgage Association—Pool Balance and Factor Report") and Telerate organizations. This monthly information, based on figures reported to GNMA by the various issuers, lists: pool number, issuer, balance (outstanding at the date cited), pool factor, rate (the stated interest rate of the pool), issue date, and maturity date.

GNMA provides a conversion factor for each pool. The factor is computed by dividing the current balance of the pool by the face amount at the time of issuance. The con-

**FIGURE 8-3**
**Monthly Factor Book**

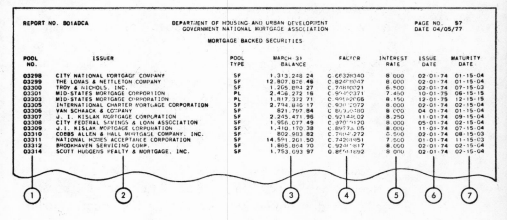

| POOL NO. | ISSUER | POOL TYPE | MARCH 31 BALANCE | FACTOR | INTEREST RATE | ISSUE DATE | MATURITY DATE |
|---|---|---|---|---|---|---|---|
| 03298 | CITY NATIONAL MORTGAGE COMPANY | SF | 1.313.248 24 | C.6F328340 | 8 000 | 02-01-74 | 01-15-04 |
| 03299 | THE LOMAS & NETTLETON COMPANY | SF | 12.807.876 46 | C.824?8047 | 8 000 | 02-01-74 | 01-15-04 |
| 03300 | TROY & NICHOLS. INC. | SF | 1.205.894 27 | C.74810021 | 6.500 | 02-01-74 | 07-15-03 |
| 03301 | MID-STATES MORTGAGE CORPORIION | PL | 2.456.272 16 | C.90402371 | 7.450 | 10-01-75 | 06-15-15 |
| 03303 | MID-STATES MORTGAGE CORPORATION | PL | 1.817.372 71 | C.99592066 | 8.150 | 12-01-75 | 12-15-15 |
| 03305 | INTERNATIONAL CHARTER MORTGAGE CORPORATION | SF | 2.794.846 17 | C.938 2072 | 8.000 | 02-01-74 | 02-15-04 |
| 03306 | VAN SCHAACK & COMPANY | SF | 821.797 84 | C.869,0480 | 8 000 | 04 01-74 | 01-15-04 |
| 03307 | J. I. KISLAK MORTGAGE CORPORATION | SF | 2.245.471 96 | 0.92144202 | 8.250 | 11-01-74 | 09-15-04 |
| 03308 | CITY FEDERAL SAVINGS & LOAN ASSOCIATION | SF | 1.956.077 49 | C.970 7120 | 8.000 | 05-01-74 | 02-15-04 |
| 03309 | J.I. KISLAK MORTGAGE CORPORATION | SF | 1.410.170 38 | C.89773.05 | 8.000 | 11-01-74 | 07-15-04 |
| 03310 | COBBS ALLEN & HALL MORTGAGE COMPANY. INC. | SF | 802.983 82 | C.7802.272 | 6.500 | 02-01-74 | 08-15-03 |
| 03311 | NATIONAL HOMES ACCEPTANCE CORPORATION | SF | 14.591.261 50 | C.74261951 | 7.500 | 01-01-74 | 11-15-03 |
| 03312 | BROOKHAVEN SERVICING CORP. | SF | 1.865.864 70 | C.9240817 | 8.000 | 02-01-74 | 02-15-04 |
| 03314 | SCOTT HUDGENS REALTY & MORTGAGE. INC. | SF | 1.753.693 97 | 0.8694-1892 | 8 000 | 02-01-74 | 02-15-04 |

REPORT NO. BO1ADCA    DEPARTMENT OF HOUSING AND URBAN DEVELOPMENT    PAGE NO. 57
GOVERNMENT NATIONAL MORTGAGE ASSOCIATION    DATE 04/05/77

MORTGAGE BACKED SECURITIES

version factor is calculated to eight decimal places. This accuracy enables the issuer to make an accurate distribution of the principal among all participants in the pool.

Multiplication of the face amount of the certificate by the eight-digit factor provides the current principal balance of the certificates.

## E. THE MONTHLY FACTOR BOOK (Figure 8-3)

1. Pool number: Number assigned by GNMA.
2. Issuer: Name of the mortgage banker servicing the pool.
3. Balance: Outstanding balance of the total pool as of the date cited.
4. Factor: Conversion factor determined by GNMA.
5. Rate: Stated interest rate of the pool.
6. Issue date: Issuance date of the original pool.
7. Maturity date: Due date for final payment on the pool.

## F. TRANSFER

Ginnie Mae securities are fully transferable and assignable. To transfer a Ginnie Mae certificate:

1. Assign the certificate in either of two ways:
   a. Complete the back, or assignment, section of the certificate (see Figure 8-2).
   b. When the registered owner does not have physical possession of the certificate, a "Special Form of Detached Assignment for United States Registered Securities" (Department of the Treasury Form PD 1832) can be filled out (see Figure 8-4). It may be used in lieu of assigning the actual certificate. (The procedure for the use of Form PD 1832 appears below.)
2. Forward the certificate to the Chemical Bank, 55 Water Street, New York, N.Y. 10041, Attention: Corporate Teller Window on Second Floor. Note: Construction loan

## FIGURE 8-4

**Form PD 1832**
Dept. of the Treasury
Bureau of the Public Debt
(Rev. Jan. 1971)

### SPECIAL FORM OF DETACHED ASSIGNMENT FOR UNITED STATES REGISTERED SECURITIES

FOR VALUE RECEIVED I assign to_____ ①

(Name)

_____
(Taxpayer identifying number and address of assignee)

the following-described registered securities of which I am (we are) the owner(s) or the duly authorized representative of
the owner: ②

TITLE OF LOAN and/or ISSUE_____

(Include interest rate, series, issue date and call and maturity dates)

| DENOMINATION | SERIAL NUMBERS | REGISTRATION (Exact inscription on each security) |
|---|---|---|
| ③ | | |
| | ④ | |
| | | ⑤ |

and hereby authorize discharge of registration thereof on the books of the Treasury Department. ⑥

_____
(Signature by or on behalf of owner)

_____
(Additional signature, if required)

I CERTIFY that the above-named person(s) as described, whose identity (or the identity of each of whom) is

well known or proved to me, personally appeared before me this_____day of_____, 19_____, ⑦

at_____ , and signed the above assignment.
(City and State)

_____ ⑧
**(SEAL)**                                  (Signature and title of certifying officer)

_____ ⑨
(Address)
*(See other side for list of officers authorized to certify assignments)*

**FIGURE 8-4** *(continued)*

## INSTRUCTIONS

> NOTE: Use of this form must be specifically authorized by a Federal Reserve Bank or Branch, the Treasurer of the United States, or the Bureau of the Public Debt.

Registered transferable securities may be assigned in blank, to bearer, to a specified transferee, to the Secretary of the Treasury for exchange for coupon securities, or to the Secretary of the Treasury for redemption or for exchange for other securities offered at maturity, upon call or pursuant to an advance refunding offer. Nontransferable securities may be assigned only in the manner and to the extent provided in the offering circulars or special applicable regulations. The owner or his authorized representative must appear before and establish his identity to the satisfaction of an officer authorized to certify assignments, and execute the assignment in the presence of that officer. The officer must then fully complete the certification form. If the securities are assigned to a specified transferee, the name, taxpayer identifying number (social security account number or employer identification number), and the address of the assignee should be shown on the form in the space provided.

### OFFICERS AUTHORIZED TO CERTIFY ASSIGNMENTS:

(1) ANY AND ALL ASSIGNMENTS:

    (a) Officers and employees of banks and trust companies chartered by or incorporated under the laws of the United States or those of any State, Commonwealth or Territory of the United States, and Federal Savings and Loan Associations, or other organizations which are members of the Federal Home Loan Bank System, who have been authorized to (i) generally bind their respective institutions by their acts, (ii) unqualifiedly guarantee signatures to assignments of securities, or (iii) expressly certify assignments of securities.

    (b) Officers of Federal Reserve Banks and Branches.

    (c) Officers of Federal Land Banks, Federal Intermediate Credit Banks and Banks for Cooperatives, the Central Bank for Cooperatives, and Federal Home Loan Banks.

    (d) United States Attorneys, Collectors of Customs, and Regional Commissioners and District Directors, Internal Revenue Service.

    (e) Judges and Clerks of United States Courts.

    (f) Commissioned and warrant officers of the Armed Forces of the United States, **but only** with respect to assignments executed by Armed Forces personnel and civilian field employees and members of the families of such personnel and civilian employees.

### CAUTION: NOTARIES PUBLIC HAVE ONLY LIMITED AUTHORITY. SEE (2) BELOW.

(2) LIMITED AUTHORITY:

Assignments for **redemption for the account of the assignor**, or for **redemption-exchange**, or pursuant to **an advance refunding offer** for other securities to be **registered in his name, or in his name with a joint owner**, may be certified by:

    (a) Justices of the peace and notaries public in the United States, its territories and possessions, the Commonwealth of Puerto Rico and the Canal Zone.

    (b) Postmasters, acting postmasters, assistant postmasters, inspectors-in-charge, chief and assistant chief accountants, and superintendents of stations of any post office in the United States, its territories and possessions, the Commonwealth of Puerto Rico and the Canal Zone.

    (c) IN **FOREIGN COUNTRIES**, ANY AND ALL ASSIGNMENTS:

        (i) United States diplomatic or consular representatives.

        (ii) Managers, assistant managers and other officers of foreign branches of banks or trust companies chartered by or incorporated under the laws of the United States or any State, Commonwealth or Territory of the United States.

        (iii) Officers authorized to administer oaths, including notaries public, but their official position and authority must be certified by the United States diplomatic or consular representative under seal of his office.

### INSTRUCTIONS TO CERTIFYING OFFICER

The owner or his authorized representative must appear before you and establish his identity to your satisfaction. The signature to the assignment or certification must be executed in your presence. Then you should fully complete and sign the certification form provided for your use.

If you are an employee (rather than an officer) authorized to certify assignments and certifications, insert the words "Authorized Signature" in the space provided for the title. Insert the place and date, as required, on the form. Impress the seal of your organization, or, if the seal is not available to you and your organization is an authorized issuing agent for Series E savings bonds, imprint the Issuing Agent's Dating Stamp in the space provided. If assignment or certification is one a notary public is authorized to certify and you are a notary, impress your seal and insert the expiration date of your commission.

certificate—CLCs—are transferable only at GNMA, Government National Mortgage Association, 451 7th Street, S.W., Washington, D.C. 20410, Attention: Secretary-Treasurer Office. Include:

a. The certificate.
b. A "letter of transfer instructions."
c. A $10 fee for each new certificate to be issued.
d. The owner's full legal name, complete address, and income tax identification number.

Instructions for filling out "Special Form of Detached Assignment for United States Registered Securities (Department of the Treasury Form PD 1832) (Figure 8-4):

1. Assignee: Name of assignee cited on back, or assignment, section of certificate.
2. Title of loan and/or issue: Full description of certificate; include date of issue, pool number, series number, interest rate, and maturity date.
3. Denomination: Original face amount of certificate.
4. Serial numbers: Number of certificate being transferred.
5. Registration: Exact inscription on certificate.
6. Assignor: Manual signature of registered certificate holder or duly appointed representative.
7. Location: Date and site of assignment.
8. Signature of witnessing officer: See instructions on reverse side of Form PD 1832.
9. Seal: Raised seal of witnessing bank or issuing agents' Series E savings bond dating stamp must be affixed here.

## G. SETTLEMENT

Settlement is an arrangement between firms and their customers for payment or receipt of cash or securities. It represents the final consummation of a securities transaction on the delivery date.

Buying transactions require the physical receipt of the actual certificate by the buyer and of federal funds by the seller. Selling transactions require the physical delivery of the actual certificates to the buyer and the receipt of federal funds by the seller.

Whether certificates are being bought or sold, they should be inspected for:

1. The pool number.
2. The rate of interest.
3. The maturity date.
4. The issuer's name.
5. The accuracy of the outstanding balance (verify by use of the factor in the monthly factor book).
6. The accuracy and completeness of the assignment on the back of the certificate.

It should be noted here that failure to make settlement on the delivery date is not in and of itself a cause for "breaking" or canceling the transaction. If circumstances beyond the control of the seller make it impossible for him to make delivery of the securities on the specified delivery date, it is customary to make settlement on the earliest possible business day. Under such circumstances the delayed settlement is made on the original figures (for accrued interest) so that the buyer is not penalized by the seller's failure to settle promptly.

## H. COLLATERAL LOANS

Pass-throughs are eligible for collateral loans. Interest rates are negotiated between the lending institutions and the borrowers.

## I. SPECIAL BUYING/TRADING METHODS

### 1. Buy for Delayed Delivery

Most new issues of Ginnie Maes are first offered for sale 15 to 60 days before the delivery date. Dealers will execute buy orders for new issues with a specific delivery date.

Prices on delayed delivery generally fluctuate in conjunction with short-term interest rates. The price differential for future deliveries depends upon the negative or positive "interest carry." For example, if short-term rates are lower than the available current yield of Ginnie Maes, future deliveries will probably be priced lower than immediates. This offsets the current return differential not earned due to delayed delivery.

During periods when short-term rates exceed those available on pass-throughs, the reverse may be true, and a delayed delivery would then sell higher than immediates.

### 2. Sell "Long for Immediate Delivery"

A long sale is one in which the seller owns the securities at the time of the sale. Such a sale is usually made for immediate delivery (an immediate) when selling portfolio securities. Profit or loss must be taken at the time of sale.

### 3. Sell "Long for Delayed Delivery"

In this transaction, portfolio securities are sold for delivery at some time in the future. Many institutions use this method of selling to plan cash requirements. This transaction can be employed to peg the price on securities which might otherwise be sold later at higher or lower prices. Mortgage bankers normally sell new issues on a "long for delayed delivery" basis.

### 4. Sell "Short for Delayed Delivery"

A short sale is one in which the seller does not own the securities at the time he sells. The seller must buy the needed securities before the committed delivery date. A variation of this transaction is "selling short against the box," in which an investor sells securities identical to those owned but with the intention of buying replacement securities before the required delivery date, rather than sell existing holdings. The "sell short for delayed delivery" transaction is used to take profits or stop losses during periods of fluctuating bond prices.

## 5. Buy under a "Standby" Commitment

A standby is an optional delivery. The purchaser or investor is paid a fee in return for a standby agreement to take delivery of the securities on a given date at a specific yield. The yield (or price), the term (time period), and the commitment fee are negotiated between the purchaser/investor and the seller/dealer of the option.

Many thrift institutions find the purchase of a standby effective because under Federal Home Loan Bank regulations they are able to take the fee into income.

## 6. Sell under a "Standby" Commitment

A nonrefundable fee is paid to an investor when he makes a commitment to take delivery of securities (at the option of the seller) on a given date. The commitment period is normally one year, but shorter or longer terms are common. The standby price ("striking" price) is negotiated.

## 7. Buy on a Repurchase Agreement

A repurchase agreement is a purchase of securities and a simultaneous agreement to resell them at a stipulated price on a specified future date. The repurchase agreement constitutes the major technique for financing dealer inventories in U.S. government and money-market securities.

## 8. Sell on a Reverse Repurchase Agreement

Securities can be converted into cash for a short period by employment of this transaction. The "reverse repo" is similar to, and often less expensive than other methods of borrowing. Portfolio securities are sold for immediate delivery and simultaneously bought back for delayed delivery. Unlike the repurchase agreement, the reverse repo is generally done for 30 days at a time and does not require the reregistering of securities.

### 9. The Swap

This transaction is a simultaneous purchase and sale of two different securities or two different issues of the same security to increase relative marketability, profit, yield, or income.

### 10. Futures Market Hedging

Hedging against the risk of interest rate changes can be done by buying or selling Ginnie Mae futures contracts on the Chicago Board of Trade as a temporary substitute for a cash-market transaction. The basic futures contract unit is a $100,000 Ginnie Mae single-family pool certificate with a stated interest rate of 8 percent. Certificates with other stated rates may be used, but they are deliverable in principal-balance amounts equivalent to $100,000 of the Ginnie Mae 8s when calculated at par and under the assumption of a 30-year certificate prepaid in its 12th year.

## J. BOOKKEEPING METHODS

Accounting is frequently subdivided into cashiering, bookkeeping, cash management, and accrual control.

The purpose of this section is to explain briefly the ease of investors' bookkeeping for Ginnie Maes. This section excludes the transfer and settlement functions, which are discussed in Sections 8.F and 8.G.

Ginnie Maes are relatively easy to administer. Investors in Ginnie Maes do not require in-house mortgage knowledge; paperwork is minimal; there is no need to examine mortgage documents, go on inspection trips, or make credit checks; legal expertise is unnecessary; no special bookkeeping techniques must be mastered. In short, Ginnie Maes are negotiable securities, and as such they can be handled quite simply.

Only four bookkeeping accounts are required: an asset account, a joint premium/discount account, an income account, and a cash account. The bookkeeping procedures can be reduced to these entries.

1. Depending on the institution, various bookkeeping practices for Ginnie Maes govern the entry of the asset value and of the asset sale.
2. Through the "Issuer's Monthly Remittance Advice" (form HUD-1714, illustrated in Figure 8-1), the proportionate application of principal and interest can be determined.
3. A single account can be used for both premiums and discounts. Thus, the premium/discount account can be amortized and debited or credited to the income account as required. A number of savings and loan associations use this single premium/discount method and amortize transactions over a ten-year period.
4. The entry for the sale of Ginnie Mae securities would, of course, be the reverse of the buy entry.

In special situations and for unique reasons, investors' accountants may recommend detailed entries. For additional information, investors should consult their accounting counsel. Savings and loan associations will find that an excellent reference source is *Standard Accounting Manual for Savings and Loan Associations,* published by the United States League of Savings Associations, 111 East Wacker Drive, Chicago, Ill. 60601.

## K. FEDERAL TAX PROVISIONS

The Internal Revenue Service has ruled:

1. A Ginnie Mae represents an undivided interest in a pool of collateralizing mortgages. The pool is regarded as a

trust. Thus these securities are qualifying assets, just as though investments were made in the underlying mortgages. (The legal eligibility of Ginnie Maes was reviewed in Section 4.F.)

Accordingly, savings banks, savings and loan associations, real estate investment trusts (REITs), and cooperative banks can invest in Ginnie Maes without jeopardizing their special tax status (e.g., deductions for bad debt reserves).

2. Investments in Ginnie Maes are regarded as "loans secured by interest in real property" under Section 7701(a)(19)(c) of the Internal Revenue Code.

3. Interest received on Ginnie Maes should be treated as ordinary income.

4. Monthly payments of principal are considered a return of capital.

5. Discounts on original issues (i.e., not market discounts) must be ratably reported as ordinary income, consistent with individual bookkeeping methods.

6. Ginnie Mae securities have no specific exemption from taxes imposed by any state or local taxing authority.

# 9

# The GNMA Mortgage-Backed Securities Dealers Associations

## A. DEALER SERVICES

Dealers in Ginnie Maes buy and sell securities for their own "principal-transactions" accounts. With their security-trading skills and financial strength (that is, invested capital and borrowing capacity), these dealers "make markets" in Ginnie Maes. (This dealer function contrasts with that of a broker who only acts as an agent or intermediary between buyers and sellers of securities.)

To assure efficient market operations, the dealers in Ginnie Maes maintain close liaison with investors so as to be continuously aware of securities available for sale and of possible bids from clients who wish to buy.

Although the various dealers have organized themselves somewhat differently, each performs these basic services:

1. Offering new securities: Originate new mortgage pools independently or in participation with others, such as dealer syndicates or mortgage bankers.
2. Trading: Provide investors with a secondary market for the Ginnie Maes they purchased. Dealers buy, sell, and take positions in or inventory these securities.

3. Settlement: Perform all necessary back office functions related to Ginnie Maes.
4. Education: Train client personnel in understanding and handling Ginnie Maes.
5. Investment advice: Assist clients in formulating and executing portfolio management strategies.

## B. HISTORY AND FUNCTIONS

To further the orderly development of the secondary market in Ginnie Maes, a small group of dealers, representing fewer than ten firms, held discussions during late 1970 and 1971. From this informal beginning, the GNMA Mortgage-Backed Securities Dealers Association was officially established on April 27, 1972. In line with the rapid growth of Ginnie Mae transactions, the number of regular and associate members has increased to over 70 since that time.

The GNMA Mortgage-Backed Securities Dealers Association is the only nationwide organization of dealers devoted exclusively to the Ginnie Mae market.

Through technical conferences and personal contacts, the association apprises its members of the present and future outlook for Ginnie Mae securities.

Members of the association are dedicated to the highest standards of professional ethics. Exacting standards of integrity and self-regulation are required of all members. These standards include knowing what types of securities are suitable for individual clients and insisting upon written confirmation of all transactions and upon well-publicized trading conventions and settlement conditions.

The association maintains a number of standing committees, including committees on trading practices, the standardization of business procedures, legal stipulations, intra- and interindustry education, and self-regulation as a specialized securities market. The activities of all standing committees are periodically reviewed by the association's executive committee.

# Exhibits

**EXHIBIT A**
Secretary of the Treasury Letter

THE SECRETARY OF THE TREASURY
WASHINGTON

FEB 13 1970

Dear Mr. Secretary:

I wish to refer to your letter of November 14, 1969
asking whether the timely payment of principal and interest
on mortgage-backed securities of the pass-through type
guaranteed by the Government National Mortgage Association
under Section 306 (g) of the National Housing Act under its
management and liquidating function is a function for which
the Association may properly borrow from the Treasury.

It is the opinion of the Treasury Department that the
Association may properly borrow from the Treasury for the
purpose of assuring the timely payment of principal and
interest on guaranteed pass-through type mortgage-backed
securities as described in Chapter 3 paragraph 6 of the
Mortgage-Backed Securities Guide dated December 1969.
Accordingly, the Treasury will make loans to the Association
for the foregoing purposes under the procedure provided in
subsection (d) of Section 306 of Title 3 of the National
Housing Act.

Sincerely,

David M Kennedy

The Honorable
George Romney
Secretary of the Department
   of Housing and Urban Development
Washington, D. C. 20410

**EXHIBIT B**
**Department of Justice Letter**

Assistant Attorney General

𝔇epartment of 𝔍ustice
𝔚ashington, 𝔇.𝔠. 20530

1969

Honorable George Romney
Secretary, Department of Housing
    and Urban Development
Washington, D. C. 20410

Dear Secretary Romney:

The Attorney General has asked me to reply to your letter to him of November 14, 1969, regarding guaranties of mortgage-backed securities proposed to be made by the Government National Mortgage Association pursuant to section 306(g) of the Federal National Mortgage Association Charter Act, as amended (12 U.S.C. (Supp. IV) 1721(g)). The proposed guaranties and the securities they would cover are described in regulations recently adopted by the Department of Housing and Urban Development. 24 CFR Part 1665. You asked whether the Association is authorized to make the proposed guaranties and whether such guaranties would be backed by the full faith and credit of the United States.

Section 306(g) of the Charter Act expressly authorizes the Association to guarantee the timely payment of principal and interest on securities described therein, and the regulations cited above conform to the statutory grant of authority. The statute provides that: "The full faith and credit of the United States is pledged to the payment of all amounts which may be required to be paid under any guaranty under this subsection." I therefore conclude that the Association is authorized to make the proposed guaranties and that they would constitute general obligations of the United States backed by its full faith and credit.

Sincerely,

William H. Rehnquist
Assistant Attorney General
Office of Legal Counsel

# Glossary

**Advance.** In real estate, a partial disbursement of funds under a note. Used most often in connection with construction lending.

**Advance commitment (conditional).** A written promise to make an investment at some time in the future if specified conditions are met.

**Allotment.** The funds allocated for the purchase of mortgages within a specified time by a permanent investor with whom a mortgage loan originator has a relationship but does not have a specific contract in the form of a commitment. The allotment may state the investor requirements as to processing, the term of the loan, and/or underwriting standards.

**Amortization.** Gradual debt reduction. Usually, the reduction is made according to a predetermined schedule for installment payments.

**Arbitrage.** The execution of two simultaneous trades, taking advantage of a spread differential that historically has been significantly different than it is at the time the trades are executed.

**Asked.** The price at which securities are offered for sale. *See* Bid and asked.

**Assignee.** The person to whom or the corporation to which an agreement or contract is assigned. One to whom real property, or an interest in real property, is transferred or set over.

**Assignment.** The transfer of a right or contract from one person to another.

**Auction.** The process by which GNMA sells mortgage-backed securities or whole loan mortgages that were held in its management and liquidation portfolio or acquired under the tandem plan.

**Backup bid.** *See* Takeout bid.

**Balloon mortgage.** A mortgage with periodic installments of principal and interest that do not fully amortize the loan. The balance of the mortgage is due in a lump sum at the end of the term.

**Balloon payment.** The unpaid principal amount of a mortgage or other long-term loan due at a certain date in the future. Usually the amount that must be paid in a lump sum at the end of the term.

**Basis point.** A measurement of changes in prices or yields for fixed income securities. One basis point equals 1/100 of 1 percent.

**Bid and asked.** Often referred to as a quotation or quote. The bid is the price one has declared that he will pay for a security at a given time; the asked is the price one will pay at the same time. *See also* Quotation, Takeout bid.

**Broker.** An agent, often a member of a stock exchange firm or an exchange member himself, who handles the public's orders to buy and sell securities or commodities and charges a commission for this service. *See also* Dealer.

**Builder Commitment.** An agreement by a lender to provide long-term financing to a builder, secured by an existing or a proposed building. The commitment usually provides for the substitution of a to-be-approved owner-occupant at a higher loan amount than has been committed to the builder.

**Building and loan association.** The name used by some savings and loan associations in a few states.

**Cash flow.** The spendable income from an investment after subtracting from gross income all operating expenses, loan payments, and the allowance for the income tax attributed to the income. The amount of cash derived over a certain measured period of time from the operation of income-producing property after debt services and operating expenses, but *before* depreciation and income taxes.

**Cheap.** Wall Street vernacular for the relative value of one security to another in terms of its historical price relationship. If a security is cheap, it is underpriced relative to another security. *See also* Rich.

**Collateral.** Securities or other property pledged by a borrower to secure repayment of a loan.

**Commitment.** An agreement to lend money to a borrower at a future date, subject to compliance with stated conditions. Applies to mortgage-backed securities. *See* Conditional commitment, Firm commitment, Standby commitment, *and* Takeout commitment.

**Commitment fee.** *See* Fee.

**Completion bond.** A bond furnished by a contractor to guarantee completion of construction.

**Conditional commitment.** A commitment (most often used with FHA loans) on a specific property for a definite loan amount with specific terms for some future purchaser of satisfactory credit standing.

**Conventional loan.** A mortgage loan made by a financial institution without government insurance or guarantee. Called a conventional loan because it conforms to accepted standards, modified within legal bounds by the mutual consent of the borrower and the lender.

**Correspondent.** A mortgage banker who services mortgage loans as a representative or agent for the mortgage owner or investor. Also applies to the mortgage banker's role as originator of mortgage loans for an investor.

**Coupon income.** The income received from the coupon rate on owned securities.

**Coupon rate.** *See* Rate of interest.

**Current yield.** Yield arrived at by dividing the coupon by the security price or cost. Often referred to as current return.

**Custodian.** When the specified amount of mortgages has been accumulated in a pool, the mortgages are submitted to an approved custodian (usually a commercial bank), which examines them. After examination and appropriate certification, GNMA issues its guaranty of the mortgage-backed security. Mortgages and related documents are held in safekeeping by the custodian.

**Dealer.** An individual or a firm in the securities business acting as a principal rather than as an agent. Typically, a dealer buys for his own account and sells to a customer from his own inventory. The dealer's profit or loss is the difference between the price he pays and the price he receives for a security. The dealer's confirmation must disclose to his customer that he has acted as a principal. At different times the same individual or firm may function as either broker or dealer.

**Default.** A breach or nonperformance of the terms of a note or the covenants of a mortgage. Usually results in foreclosure.

**Department of Housing and Urban Development.** *See* HUD.

**Disintermediation.** The phenomenon that occurs when the rates being paid by certain financial intermediaries cannot compete with the rates being paid by others (e.g., the U.S. government on its Treasury bills). This causes a shrinkage in the amount of deposits held by those financial intermediaries which are unable to pay the higher rates. *See also* Intermediation.

**Due bill.** A corporate promissory note delivered to a customer by a broker or dealer in lieu of securities. A due bill must be replaced by actual securities at a later date.

**Eligibility.** *See* Legal eligibility.

**Endorsement.** A writing on a negotiable instrument by which title to property mentioned therein is assigned and transferred. A notation added to an instrument after execution to change or clarify its contents.

**Escrow.** A transaction in which a third party, acting as an agent for the buyer and the seller, carries out the instructions of both and assumes the responsibilities of handling the paperwork and the disbursement of funds.

**Escrow fees.** Fees charged by the escrow holder for his services.

**Escrow payment.** That portion of a mortgagor's monthly payments held in trust by the lender to pay for taxes, hazard insurance, mortgage insurance, lease payments, and other items as they become due. Known in some states as impounds.

**Face value.** The value of a bond or similar security that appears on the face of the certificate. Ordinarily the amount the issuer promises to pay at maturity. Face value is not an indication of market value. Sometimes referred to as par value. Refers to the original principal amount of mortgage-backed securities.

**Fannie Mae.** Nickname. *See* Federal National Mortgage Association (FNMA).

**Farmers Home Administration (FmHA).** A government agency established under the Farmers Home Administration Act of 1946 to provide financing to farmers and other qualified borrowers who are unable to obtain loans elsewhere. It makes, participates in, and insures loans for rural housing and other purposes.

**Federal association.** A savings association chartered and regulated by the Federal Home Loan Bank Board.

**Federal Home Loan Bank (FHLB).** One of the 12 federally chartered regional banks of the Federal Home Loan Bank System. A primary function of the Home Loan banks is to supply credit to member institutions.

**Federal Home Loan Bank Board (FHLBB).** A regulatory and supervisory agency for federally chartered savings institutions. Oversees the operations of the Federal Savings and Loan Insurance Corporation and the Federal Home Loan Mortgage Corporation.

**Federal Home Loan Mortgage Corporation (FHLMC).** A private corporation authorized by Congress. FHLMC is a secondary-market facility of the FHLB system. It sells participation sales certificates secured by pools of conventional mortgage loans whose principal and interest are guaranteed by the federal government through the FHLMC. It has also sold GNMA bonds to raise funds to finance the purchase of mortgages. Popularly known as Freddie Mac.

**Federal Housing Administration (FHA).** A division of HUD. Its main activity is the insuring of residential mortgage loans made by private lenders. It sets standards for construction and underwriting. FHA does not lend money or construct housing.

**Federal National Mortgage Association (FNMA).** A taxpaying corporation created by Congress to support the secondary mortgage market. It purchases and sells residential mortgages insured by FHA or guaranteed by VA, as well as conventional home mortgages.

**Federal Savings and Loan Insurance Corporation (FSLIC).** An instrumentality of the federal government which insures the savings accounts in member savings and loan associations.

**Fee.** (1) Commitment fee: a payment to investors or prospective investors, which may or may not be refundable, for the purpose of obtaining a commitment to purchase securities; (2) standby fee: a nonrefundable amount received or paid for the sale or purchase of a standby commitment; (3) up-front fee: a commitment fee paid in advance of the settlement date to an investor as part of a future purchase.

**Financial intermediary.** A financial institution which acts as an intermediary between savers and borrowers by accepting money from the public and, in turn, lending the accumulated funds to borrowers. The classification includes savings associations, commercial banks, mutual savings banks, life insurance companies, and credit unions.

**Firm commitment.** A lender's agreement to make a loan to a specific borrower on a specific property. An FHA or conventional mortgage agreement to insure a loan on a specific property, with a designated borrower.

**Foreclosure.** An authorized procedure taken by a mortgagee or lender, under the terms of a mortgage or a deed of trust, for the purpose of having the property applied to the payment of a defaulted debt.

**Foreclosure payment.** A prepayment made to holders of mortgage-backed securities from proceeds of property liquidation after foreclosure. Amount of prepayment must equal the principal balance of the foreclosed mortgage.

**Funding date.** Term used by mortgage bankers to denote the date on which the mortgage banker funds or finances a new issue of Ginnie Maes. *See also* Settlement date.

**GI loan.** Colloquial term for a mortgage loan guaranteed by the VA.

**Ginnie Mae mortgage-backed securities (or Ginnie Maes).** Securities guaranteed by GNMA and issued by mortgage bankers, commercial banks, savings and loan associations, savings banks, and other institutions. The Ginnie Mae security holder is protected by the full faith and credit of the U.S. government. Ginnie Mae securities are backed by FHA, VA, or FmHA mortgages. The term *pass-throughs* is often used to describe Ginnie Maes.

**Government National Mortgage Association (GNMA).** On September 1, 1968, Congress enacted legislation to partition FNMA into two continuing corporate entities. GNMA assumed responsibility for the special assistance loan program and the management and liquidation functions of the older FNMA. GNMA also administers and guarantees mortgage-backed securities which channel new sources of funds into residential financing through the sale of privately issued mortgage-backed securities.

**Guaranteed loan.** Usually applies to a loan guaranteed by VA, FmHA, or any other interested party.

**Guaranty.** A promise by one party to pay a debt or perform an obligation contracted by another party in the event that the original obligor fails to pay or perform as contracted. The full faith and credit of the U.S. government is pledged to the payment of all amounts which GNMA may be required to pay under the terms of its guaranty. GNMA has complete authority to borrow from the Treasury in order to meet its obligations under the guaranty.

**Housing starts.** *See* Starts.

**HUD.** The Department of Housing and Urban Development. Established by the Housing and Urban Development Act of 1965 to supersede the Housing and Home Finance Agency. Responsible for the implementation and administration of government housing and urban development programs. HUD programs include community planning and development, housing production, the extension of mortgage credit (FHA), and ensuring equal opportunity in housing.

**Impound.** *See* Escrow payment.

**Income property.** Real estate developed or improved to produce income.

**Institutional lender.** A financial institution that invests in mortgages and carries them in its own portfolio. Mutual savings banks, life insurance companies, commercial banks, pension and trust funds, and savings and loan associations are examples.

**Insured association.** A savings association whose savings accounts are insured by FSLIC.

**Insured loan.** A loan insured by FHA or a private mortgage insurance company.

**Interest rate.** *See* Rate of interest.

**Intermediation.** The phenomenon that occurs when rates paid by certain financial intermediaries can compete successfully with the rates being paid by others (e.g., the U.S. government on its Treasury bills). This causes an expansion in the amount of deposits held by the intermediaries which are able to pay higher rates. *See also* Disintermediation.

**Issuer.** One who issues securities, usually a mortgage banker who pools mortgages to back GNMA pass through securities. *See* Originator.

**Legal eligibility.** A term describing investments that life insurance companies, mutual savings banks, or other regulated investors may make under a state charter, law or regulation.

**Liquidity.** Considered an attribute of marketability. *See* Marketability.

**Liquidity portfolio.** That portion of a savings and loan association's assets which is kept in short-term securities (maturity of five years or less). Federal savings and loans are required to keep a certain proportion of their assets in a liquidity portfolio; the percentage, established by the FHLBB, is subject to change.

**Loan submission.** A package of pertinent papers and documents regarding a property or properties. It is delivered by a would-be borrower or his agent to a prospective lender for review and consideration for the purpose of obtaining a mortgage loan. Once an FHA/FmHA or VA loan is closed, these papers become part of the loan package which also includes the note, mortgage or deed of trust, title policy and certificate of insurance or guarantee.

**Margin.** The amount paid by the customer when he uses his broker's credit to buy a security. Under Federal Reserve regulations, the initial margin required is subject to change from time to time.

**Market order.** An order to buy or sell a stated amount of a security at the most advantageous price obtainable after the order is entered.

**Market price.** In the case of a security, market price is usually considered the last reported price at which the security sold.

**Marketability.** The capacity of the market in a particular security to absorb a reasonable amount of buying and selling at reasonable price changes. The degree of investment interest underlying a security. Marketability largely determines the value of a security in the marketplace. Liquidity is considered an attribute of marketability. A Ginnie Mae possesses a high degree of marketability due to the existence of large, active primary (new supply) and secondary (trading) markets. It is also a negotiable security. *See* Negotiable security.

**Maturity.** The terminating or due date of a note, time draft, acceptance, bill of exchange, mortgage-backed security, or bond. The date a time instrument of indebtedness becomes due and payable.

**Mortgage.** A conveyance of an interest in real property given as security for the payment of a debt. In some states, a deed of trust.

**Mortgage-backed securities.** *See* Ginnie Mae mortgage-backed securities.

**Mortgage banker.** A company that specializes in originating mortgage loans for sale to permanent investors. It frequently continues to service the loans it has sold. As the local representative of regional or national institutional lenders, it acts as a correspondent between lenders and borrowers.

**Mortgage banking.** The packaging of mortgage loans secured by real property to be pooled to back issues of Ginnie Mae securities or sold to a permanent investor, with servicing retained for the life of the loan. The origination, sale, and servicing of mortgage loans by a firm or an individual. The investor-correspondent system is the foundation of the mortgage banking industry.

**Mortgage broker.** An agent who brings the borrower and the lender together, receiving a commission. A mortgage broker does not perform the servicing function.

**Mortgage insurance premium (MIP).** The consideration paid by a mortgagor for mortgage insurance, either to FHA or a private mortgage insurance (PMI) company. On an FHA loan, the payment is one half of 1 percent annually on the declining balance of the mortgage. It is a part of the regular monthly payment and is used by FHA to meet operating expenses and provide loss reserves.

**Mortgagee.** The institution, group, or person to whom property is conveyed as collateral for a loan made by such person or firm (a creditor).

**Mortgagor.** The borrower who receives funds in a mortgage transaction.

**Negotiable security.** Under the UCC (*see* Uniform Commercial Code), an instrument that meets certain legal requirements and can be transferred by endorsement or delivery. A Ginnie Mae is assignable and transferable, hence a negotiable security.

**Net yield.** The part of gross yield that remains after the deductions of all costs, such as mortgage servicing expenses and guaranty fees. *See also* Yield.

**Origination.** The process whereby a Ginnie Mae certificate, backed by approved mortgages in a pool, is issued.

**Originator.** One whose function is to originate or issue mortgage-backed securities. Builders, brokers, and others are solicited to obtain applications for mortgage loans. The individual mortgage banker who performs this function is also designated as the originator or issuer.

**Participation certificate.** A type of mortgage-backed security which represents an undivided interest in certain real estate loans.

**Participation loan.** (1) A mortgage made by one lender in which one or more other lenders own a part interest; (2) a mortgage originated by two or more lenders.

**Pass-throughs.** *See* Ginnie Mae mortgage-backed securities.

**Permanent investor.** One who provides permanent mortgage financing.

**Pipeline.** Term used by mortgage bankers to describe the amount or number of mortgages they have in process but have not actually closed.

**Point.** An amount equal to 1 percent of the principal amount of an investment or note. Loan discount points are a one-time charge assessed at closing by the lender to increase the yield on the mortgage loan to a competitive position.

**Premium.** The amount by which a security may sell above its face value. In the case of a new issue, the amount that the market price rises over the original selling price. Also refers to a charge sometimes made when a security is borrowed to make delivery on a short sale. May also refer to the redemption price of a security if that price is higher than the security's face value.

**Prepayment.** Partial or complete payment of a mortgage by a mortgagor due to such circumstances as a change in family size, moving, the sale of the mortgagor's home, or the death of the mortgagor. *See also* Default, Foreclosure.

**Primary market.** Offerings in newly issued Ginnie Maes. *See also* Secondary market.

**Principal balance.** The outstanding balance of a mortgage, exclusive of interest and any other charges.

**Principal transaction.** A securities transfer wherein one or both of the parties act as principals dealing for their own account.

**Privately insured mortgage.** A conventional mortgage loan on which a private mortgage insurance company protects the lender against a portion of the loss.

**Private mortgage insurance (PMI).** Insurance written by a private company protecting the mortgage lender against a portion of the loss occasioned by a mortgage default.

**Quality.** A security is said to be of high quality if the return of principal and payment of interest are well secured or guaranteed.

**Quotation.** The bid to buy and the offer to sell a security in a given market at a given time. Often shortened to "quote." *See also* Bid and asked.

**Rate of interest.** Annual interest rate of a pool; the coupon rate. Not necessarily the same as yield.

**Real estate owned (REO).** A term frequently applied by lending institutions to the ownership of real property acquired for investments or as a result of foreclosure.

**Real estate syndicate.** A group of investors who pool funds for investment in real property.

**Realtor®.** A real estate broker or an associate holding active membership in a local real estate board affiliated with the National Association of Realtors. A registered term.

**Realty.** Real property and the business of buying and selling real property.

**Redemption period.** The time during which some states allow a foreclosed mortgagor to buy back his property by paying the amount owed, including interest and fees. The originator or issuer of Ginnie Maes is responsible for maintaining normal monthly payments during a redemption period.

**Reinstatement.** The acknowledgment by a mortgagee that an accelerated loan has been brought current by the mortgagor.

**Repurchase agreement (Repo).** The selling of securities by a dealer to another party at the same time that the other party enters into an agreement to resell the securities to the dealer on a delayed settlement basis; basically a financing transaction.

**Reserves.** That portion of a company's earnings which has been set aside to take care of possible losses in the conduct of business; listed in the balance sheet as a liability.

**Reverse repurchase agreement (Reverse Repo).** The purchase of securities by a dealer from another party at the same time that the other party enters into an agreement to repurchase the securities from the dealer on a delayed settlement basis. A collateralized borrowing.

**Rich.** Wall Street vernacular for the relative value of one security to another in terms of its historical price relationship. If a security is rich, it is overpriced relative to another security. *See also* Cheap.

**Safety.** An attribute of an investment. Safety is often associated with securities that are insured or guaranteed.

**Savings and loan association.** A financial intermediary which accepts savings from the public and invests those savings, mainly in mortgage loans. Always a corporation but may be either a mutual or a capital stock institution and may be either state-chartered or federally chartered (with the term *federal* used in its name). A "stock association" is a state-chartered savings and loan association with some form of capital stock ownership.

**Savings bank (mutual).** State-chartered financial institutions that have investment powers somewhat broader than savings and loan associations.

**Secondary market.** The resale market for securities. *See also* Primary market.

**Secondary mortgage market.** The total buying, selling, and trading of existing mortgage loans and of participations in such loans. Contrasts with the primary mortgage market, in which mortgages are originated.

**Security.** A common or preferred stock, a bond, a U.S. government or agency issue, or a state or municipal obligation. (In real estate practice, security represents the collateral given, deposited, or pledged to secure the fulfillment of an obligation or the payment of a debt.) *See also* Negotiable security.

**Seller-servicer.** The term for an approved corporation that sells mortgages to, and services mortgages for FNMA and/or GNMA.

**Servicing.** The duties of the mortgage banker as a loan correspondent, per specifications in the servicing agreement for which a fee is received. The collection for an investor of payments, interest, principal, and trust items, such as hazard insurance and taxes, on a note by the borrower in accordance with the terms of the note. Servicing also consists of operational procedures covering accounting, bookkeeping, insurance, tax records, loan payment follow-up, delinquency loan follow-up, and loan analysis.

**Servicing agreement.** A written agreement between an investor and a mortgage loan correspondent stipulating the rights and obligations of each party.

**Settlement date.** The date agreed upon by parties to a security transaction for the actual payment of funds and transfer of the security. Mortgage bankers sometimes use this term to indicate a settlement on mortgages.

**Short sale.** The seller anticipates that the price for the security he has sold short (i.e., borrowed) will decline to a certain level. When that price level is reached, he buys the security, thereby "covering" the short. *See also* Long.

**Spot loans.** Single-family loans solicited on an individual basis.

**Standby commitment.** In Ginnie Mae trading, a standby represents a *put,* exercisable at a future date; the holder of a standby commitment has the right, but not the obligation, to make delivery. *See also* Striking price.

**Standby fee.** *See* Fee.

**Starts.** A term commonly used to indicate the number of residential units whose construction has begun within a stated period of time. Often referred to as "housing starts."

**Street name.** A registered security which has been endorsed in blank or endorsed in favor of a recognized dealer is said to be in street name.

**Striking price.** The price at which Ginnie Mae securities can be sold upon the exercise of a standby commitment. *See also* Standby commitment.

**Swap.** The simultaneous purchase and sale of two different securities or two different issues of the same security to increase relative marketability, profit, yield, or income.

**Takeout bid.** A GNMA dealer agrees to purchase Ginnie Mae securities at a specific price from a mortgage banker subject to a successful bid for mortgages sold at auction. This takeout or *backup bid* allows the mortgage banker to bid on the purchase of mortgages at a GNMA whole loan auction. The dealer's takeout bid permits the mortgage banker to add a bulk purchase of mortgages, obtained from GNMA, to his servicing portfolio. This two-party agreement helps GNMA to implement its management and liquidation functions. In net effect, the mortgage banker is purchasing the mortgage collateral and is financially backed by the Ginnie Mae dealer.

**Takeout commitment.** A promise to make a loan at a specified time. It is most commonly used to designate a higher-cost, shorter-term backup commitment as a support for construction financing until a suitable permanent loan can be secured.

**TBA.** Future Ginnie Mae pools "to be announced" which are bought and sold for future settlement. "To be announced" refers to interest rates and due dates, which are determined when available. Trading in these securities is often done on a yield basis.

**Term.** The period of time between the commencement date and the termination date of a note, mortgage, legal document, or other contract.

**Trade.** The term applied to either a purchase or a sale of a security.

**Trading.** The act of carrying out purchasing and/or selling in a security or a securities market.

**Trading income.** Income derived from the trading of a portfolio of securities.

**Trading profits or losses.** Profits or losses resulting from the trading of a portfolio of securities.

**Transfer agent.** A transfer agent keeps a record of the name of each registered shareowner, his or her address, and the number of certificates he or she owns, and sees that certificates presented to the transfer agent's office for transfer are properly canceled and that new certificates are issued in the name of the transferee.

**Underwriting.** Securities dealers use this term to designate the issue or origination of new securities. Mortgage bankers generally use the term to indicate the analysis of risk and the matching of risk to an appropriate rate and term.

**Uniform Commercial Code (UCC).** A comprehensive law regulating commercial transactions. It has been adopted, with modification, by most states.

**Up-front fee.** *See* Fee.

**Variable rate mortgage.** A mortgage agreement that allows for adjustment of the interest rate in keeping with a fluctuating market and with terms agreed upon in the note.

**Veterans Administration (VA).** An independent agency of the federal government created by the Servicemen's Readjustment Act of 1944 to administer a variety of benefit programs designed to facilitate the adjustment of returning veterans to civilian life. The VA home loan guaranty program is designed to encourage lenders to offer long-term, low-down-payment mortgages to eligible veterans by guaranteeing the lenders against loss. The VA also guarantees mobile home loans to eligible veterans.

**Warehousing.** The borrowing of funds by a mortgage banker on a short-term basis at a commercial bank, using permanent mortgage loans as collateral. This form of interim financing is used until the mortgages are sold to a permanent investor. It is a form of "line of credit" financing.

**Whole loans.** Mortgages which have not been pooled to back mortgage-backed securities or participation certificates are often referred to as being whole loans.

**Yield.** The yield on a bond is the annual percentage of return that it pays. In real estate, the term refers to the effective annual amount of income which is being accrued on an investment, expressed as a percentage of the price originally paid. *See also* Net yield.

**Yield on average life.** Ginnie Mae yields are quoted from tables which calculate the yield on a single loan prepaid at the end of 12 years. It is assumed that such a yield calculation is fairly representative of a pool of loans wherein the average loan life is thought to be 12 years. This is not a guarantee of investment results, but an accepted practice for trading Ginnie Maes and mortgages in secondary markets. The "12-year average life" convention is based largely upon FHA statistics.

**Yield to maturity.** A percentage returned each year to the lender on actual funds borrowed, considering that the loan will be paid in full at maturity.